Endorsements

Carlie has done an amazing job of combining her miraculous testimony with sharing revelations from God's Word of who we are and what we have in Christ. She shares tragic events from her life with a humor that keeps your attention and yet drives the truths home.

It's been my privilege to know the whole Terradez family since 2006 and minister with them on many different occasions. They are called and anointed by the Lord, and I know you will be encouraged and challenged as I was by reading this book. God is no respecter of persons (Romans 2:11). What He has done for Carlie, He will do for you.

Andrew Wommack
President and Founder of Andrew Wommack Ministries
and Charis Bible College

Carlie Terradez is a rare person and dear friend. We have ministered together on several occasions, and I can tell you she is the real deal.

All Is Not Lost is Carlie's journey from victim to champion. She knows the value of true redemption and carries an urgency to reach those caught in darkness. Her bravery and raw transparency should be applauded.

I highly recommend this book! It is a must read, especially for anyone desiring to live a delivered life! You will find hope and the promise of a better tomorrow.

I'm proud of you for writing this, sister!

Heather Z
Speaker, Broadcaster

Another powerful book by Carlie! *All Is Not Lost* is real, vulnerable, and so needed in these times we are living in. Many people know the Word of God but don't see the power of it activated in their lives. Carlie "puts herself out there" with her own life examples to show us a way out of any pit and how to activate the power of God's Word! I know God will use this book to set you free and begin to see signs, wonders and miracles in your own life!

Kara Diaz
Pastor, Author, Speaker

All

IS NOT

Lost

Harrison House

Shippensburg, PA

Other Books by Carlie Terradez

Fearless: Breaking the Habit of Fear

Miracles & Healing Made Easy: Inspiring Stories of Faith

Hannah and the Beanstalk! A True Story of Faith

Also from Terradez Ministries:

Thorns, Barns, and Oil Jars by Ashley Terradez

God Wants You Rich by Ashley Terradez

*Your Life with God: What it Means to Be Born Again
and Receive the Baptism of the Holy Spirit*

*39 Reasons Healing is Yours: Healing Scriptures
that Beat Sickness to Death*

Carul x

All

IS NOT Lost

YOUR PATH FROM
TRAUMA TO VICTORY

Published by Harrison House Publishers
Shippensburg, PA 17257

ISBN 13 TP: 978-1-6803-1956-9

ISBN 13 eBook: 978-1-6803-1957-6

For Worldwide Distribution, Printed in the U.S.A.

1 2 3 4 5 6 7 8 / 26 25 24 23 22

Contents

Foreword

by Dr. Doug Weiss

Rarely do you meet someone who has been part of raising the dead. However, in this book, not only will you get to meet Carlie, but you will sincerely get to know her. Few have raised people from the dead, but it is exceptionally rare to have an opportunity like this where you can dive deep into someone like Carlie's personal journey that helped shape her into who she is today.

Carlie has experienced many obstacles on her journey, including trauma and crippling sickness, but she shares an incredible redemption story—your past does not need to define your future!

This book introduces you to Carlie's past struggles as she (literally) took one step at a time to climb a mountain. She vulnerably shares her challenges and how she conquered these obstacles in her own life.

As you read through these pages, Carlie will take your hand and heart like a close friend or caring family member and walk you through the biblical process of allowing God to show you who He is during these challenging times.

All Is Not Lost is a paradigm-shifting book that will take you through the strengthening process of overcoming fear, grief, trauma, pain, and other obstacles along your journey.

Reading this book brought overwhelmingly powerful images to my head from the Marvel movie, *Iron Man*. In this movie, Tony Stark can push a button and his armor surrounds his body, protecting him from anyone or anything that wishes to harm him.

Similarly, this book will help you add armor, strategies, and weapons that can help you face the challenges from your past, present or future. Carlie will be your guide as you read this manual about truly living a supernatural life.

As you read through these pages, I recommend you absorb and practice these strategies in your day-to-day life, and the difficulties in front of you will submit to the Spirit of God that dwells in you richly.

Doug Weiss, Ph.D.
Executive Director of Heart to Heart Counseling Center
Colorado Springs, Colorado

Prologue

Sometimes life just stinks! Bad things happen to good people. Life is not fair.

While these statements are true, and I know that they have left my lips at times, none of them bring hope or healing. Life does not discriminate; it happens every day to everyone regardless of wealth, position, education, gender, or skin color. Then life goes on, regardless of whether we feel able to handle it or not. We may not have a choice in some of the events life throws our way, but we do have a choice in how we respond to them.

The Bible is full of examples of those who faced overwhelming obstacles—physical and emotional—yet overcame them with the wisdom, power, and faith of God. When David ran at Goliath, he did so with a confidence that caused him to shout, with a boldness that smacked of faith and struck fear in the heart of the enemy. While everyone around him was paralyzed with the fear of defeat, David faced the same challenge but responded with victory already in his mind.

How was it that David saw the same giant as everyone else but faced it so differently? David knew that the power of God in him was greater than any obstacle in his way, that his fate was not determined by the circumstances around him nor based on his ability to overcome them. No. His victory was already settled. His victory went ahead of him because he knew the Lord was with him.

That is the kind of faith we need to walk in victory in this life. The kind that rejoices in the middle of a disaster because it has seen the victory on the other side. I know this is possible because it's in the Bible! If Jesus really is the same yesterday, today, and forever, that means God's promises are as fresh and available to us today as they have ever been (Hebrews 13:8).

There is a path David took that led him from the point of staring death in the face—as a shepherd, not a soldier—to chopping off the head of that ugly giant and feeding it to the birds. It's the path of the underdog. You have to watch out for the underdog because no one expects him to win, and just at the point where it looks like all is lost, something unexpected happens…

The victorious underdog responds to challenges in ways that defy what most of humanity considers to be normal. So, what is the correct response when faced with bad news, when tragedy strikes, or when loss feels like it is consuming every cell in your body? Where is the ladder to lead us out of the pit in which we find ourselves when our hearts are broken? When everything looks lost, how do we get back on the path and become found again?

If while examining your situation it looks like all is lost, you are reading the right book! The darkest time of the night is right before the dawn. In fact, we can face the dark in *anticipation* of the light.

Walk with me awhile on your path from trauma to victory. I'm going to be honest with you and expose some of the raw parts of me because I believe there is a victor inside every victim who is just itching to get out. I believe that the very darkest parts of our souls can give birth to the most amazing comebacks! What the devil may have sent to destroy you might just be his biggest failure—and *your* greatest victory.

What the devil may have sent to destroy you might just be his biggest failure—and your greatest victory.

Chapter One

A Bad Day for the Devil

Muffled gasps fluttered through the air, whispers turned into chatter, and a growing unrest blew through the crowded auditorium.

I didn't see the woman at first. Approaching from my right through the darkness of the room against the brightness of the stage lights, I wasn't aware of her until she laid the child on the stage beside me.

No one knew of this mother's struggle—how could they? She was a stranger among the thousands who came that day. However, like the woman with the issue of blood, this mother pushed her way through the crowds to make her way to Jesus.

In her arms she carried her infant son. Her journey there had been long and filled with a mixture of desperation and tentative expectation. Walking down the aisle toward the stage that morning, the battle was on to determine which of these emotions would overcome.

The expectation and hope had launched this family on their cross-country journey. Days in the car with the whole family on a road trip can be a test under the best of circumstances, but this was no simple family outing; this was a make-or-break, life-altering determination to take possession of a promise.

> *I shall not die, but live, And declare the works of the Lord.*
>
> Psalm 118:17

They came with an assignment: to grasp ahold of healing for their son, for their baby brother. As they loaded the family car with the children and prepared for the thousands of miles ahead of them, all they had was their faith in God. And that was all that they needed.

Their faith in God was all they needed.

> *Jesus answered and said to them, "Have faith in God."*
>
> Mark 11:22

The journey was long and difficult, filled with opportunities to give room to fear. But what other options were there? Stay home and wait for death to take its young victim, for the grief of a lost child to consume their family?

Going on in faith was the only option this mother was prepared to consider. Healing was waiting for them, and her own heart was placing a demand on it.

> *Then He touched their eyes, saying, "According to your faith let it be to you." And their eyes were opened…*
>
> Matthew 9:29-30

Healing for their son was at that conference, and no obstacle in their way would stop them from getting there. No one there knew their story, the heartache they had already endured. To everyone else, they looked like any other family.

As the mother laid her precious son on the stage at my feet, her words were barely audible, "Please help me, my baby is not breathing."

This was about to be a *really* bad day for the devil. I knew it.

Death Has No Sting

Earlier that morning, as I awoke, there had been a scripture on my lips:

ALL IS NOT LOST

Whom God raised up, having loosed the pains of death,
because it was not possible that He should be held by it.

Acts 2:24

Death did not have the power to hold Jesus in the grave, it was powerless against Him. If it could have kept Him there it would have, but death had lost its grip. It struck me that morning: if death did not have power back then, surely it has no power now.

If death did not have power back then, surely it has no power now.

Jesus defeated death itself. The very end result of sickness and disease people fear the most had been crushed. If no sickness is greater than death itself, and that had been overcome, then no sickness—regardless of its prognosis—could stay in a body and live.

Death has truly lost its sting!

My drive to the conference that morning was different. Brought back to my remembrance were the dreams of the previous few nights, all different, yet somehow the same. Over and over, I saw people being raised from the dead in my sleep.

Old people, young people, different circumstances, different nationalities, yet the same devil behind the death and the same Jesus overruling it! My confession until then had been that I had never been in a position to see a person raised from the dead, but that I had often dreamed about it.

Goldfish-Raising Power

Goldfish, however, were another matter. The goldfish was doomed from the get-go, being no match for a two-year-old who insisted on feeding the unfortunate creature his orange juice. Absent of an official autopsy, I'm relatively certain that the cause of death was toddler-initiated poisoning.

After three days, I finally got around to scooping the slimy, decaying fish out of tank. He was more than a little green around the gills and the very distinctive odor of death filled the air.

Flopping the fish from the net onto the counter, it occurred to me that Jesus viewed death a little differently than we do. To Him, it's not such a big deal. Was it really that big of an issue that this fish was dead? Was he truly destined to die prematurely at the hand of an inexperienced aquarist? Was it too late for him?

My finger found its way to the fish's distended belly, and gently pressed a few times. Feeling foolish, realizing I was attempting CPR on a three-day-dead fish, I swiftly drew the line at attempting mouth-to-mouth resuscitation!

I recalled that when He had been faced with a dead girl, Jesus had an entirely different technique. He didn't try chest compressions. Instead, He spoke to the problem: "Little girl, arise!"

Soooo, I figured if it worked for Jesus, it was worth a shot.

"Little fish, arise!" I commanded.

Gradually, his color began to change from green to orange and its tail fin began to flop up and down! Our dead fish was now very much alive! I plopped him in some fresh water right away. He went on to live for several more years, eventually dying of more natural causes.

Our dead fish was now very much alive!

For someone who, at the time, knew very little about faith and how it worked, I learned that day to view death as temporary.

Death Is Temporary

I didn't realize how significant that lesson was until I held that cold, motionless baby in my arms years later.

Death was back. It still smelled the same. Only, this time, the stakes were infinitely higher, the cost much greater. Yet the smell of death wasn't accompanied by the usual fear or panic, rushing to call first responders. Death was still temporary—the atmosphere was one of peace.

Time seemed to stop. Everything in my senses went quiet. The peace of God enveloped the small group of speakers praying on the stage and drew in the eyes of the crowd. The Holy Spirit had something to say:

Hush, this child is not dead but sleeping.

As I scooped the little boy up in my arms, his head fell backward, and his big brown eyes rolled back in their sockets until only the whites were showing. His chubby little arms were outstretched like a starfish and hung limp. His chest had stopped moving; he wasn't breathing.

As a former nurse, I instinctively checked for his pulse but felt nothing. His lips were gray, and an ashen tone covered his brown skin. Yet, giving this baby CPR didn't even occur to me. Instead, I heard the Holy Spirit's voice again.

He is not dead but sleeping. This is temporary. Now, speak to it.

"Life, in Jesus' name! Heart, beat; brain, function." Authority resonated up from my spirit and I felt it leave my lips in those words.

Good. Now slap the death out of him.

One swift, solid tap on his side and suddenly life entered his little body. Immediately, the baby's arms reached up toward me

ALL IS NOT LOST

and his eyes, rolling back into place, caught mine. He gasped, taking in oxygen like someone who had just surfaced from deep water.

The peace of God felt heavy, like a deep rest was settling about us. I held the little one in my arms for a few moments, feeling the warmth return to his body. His eyes grew heavy; he had just experienced quite the adventure! As if nothing was ever out of the ordinary, blissfully unaware of the thousands of onlookers, he fell asleep in my arms.

Turning to his mother, I gently transferred the sleeping baby back into her arms.

"It's ok now. He's just sleeping," I explained.

As we made our way back up the steps to the stage, the small group of speakers reassembling to carry on with the teaching, it was only then that I noticed the father of the baby and their other children who had been standing behind us watching the whole event unfold.

Victory Is Normal

It wasn't until later—all of us backstage debriefing the morning's events, and when Andrew Wommack said, "Well, we just saw a baby raised from the dead"—when it truly occurred to me what had happened. It all had just seemed so normal, so natural, like death never had a chance. We had the advantage all along. The battle had already been won before we even knew we were in one!

God is always supernatural, but He is rarely spectacular. We can miss the supernatural in looking for the spectacular. He is always with us, not just when we feel Him, or hear Him speak, or see Him working in a supernatural way. No. He is always with us.

> *We can miss the supernatural in looking for the spectacular.*

In the times when we have lost our way, in the moments when we are angry at Him, at life, at the world, He is there. When faith is like a mystery that we can't figure out or are frightened to even try, and when we are too tired to believe because our heart is hurting from the grief of previous disappointments. He is with us even then, protecting us from harm that we didn't see, deafening our ears to words that would hurt us, guarding our hearts with His peace.

This event was not a coincidence. This victory was prepared years in advance before that baby was ever born. It was a predetermined win. God had already planned the victory parade before we ever saw the battle.

Imagine that: a Father who cares so much for His child that He prepares a way of escape from the clutches of death before the child's existence. God is way more faithful to keep His Word than we can fathom.

...What can man do to me?

Hebrews 13:6

Chapter Two

Saved and Lost

That Sunday evening service was sparse. None of the other youth had made it, so I found myself sitting alone in the pew. It was quiet, and my mind wandered, unable to focus on the vicar's sermon about seven candlesticks in the book of Revelation and their significance to my life. No, I was busy just trying to survive.

As I sat on that red velvet pew cushion in my cut off denim jeans and ripped t shirt with rainbow lettering (that was before the rainbow meant anything more than a rainbow), my eighteen-year life began to replay in my mind. So many parts of it had been off limits. I tried not to think about some of the more traumatic aspects of my childhood.

As the movie played in my mind, I couldn't have cared less about the conversation I'd just had with a disgruntled deacon about my attire. I didn't know—it wasn't like I was trying to upset anyone by violating their unwritten dress code. I just came as I was because Jesus told me that was just fine.

Sitting in church as a year-old believer, I didn't have a clue what the vicar was talking about. It may as well have been Latin.

In church, we speak a whole different language than the world outside. The first time I heard the word *sin* was in church. Until then, I just thought Jesus loved me! (He *does* love me, regardless of my sin; this I now know.)

I was saved, yes, but I was also totally lost. I know that sounds messed up, but I *was* messed up! I had said the sinner's prayer and secured my spot in heaven alright, but my life didn't look much different from my heathen neighbor's. I was sick, I was broken, and I was hiding behind a mask that I put on for church, hoping no one could see through to what was behind it.

I was not the only one.

Now I can clearly see church masks everywhere. We can see people putting on their church masks in the parking lot. It's amazing what happens on a Sunday when you are trying to get everyone out of the house, looking somewhat decent with matching socks, faces free from breakfast remnants, and ensuring the dog hair remains on the dog rather than on you!

As an adult, I finally gave up on church masks with the arrival of child number three and counted it a successful morning if we all made it to church alive, and fully clothed, before the end of worship. The truth is, no one has it all together, or rolls out of bed with their hair fixed, make-up on, kids perfectly behaved, and husband basking in his wife's glorious ability to create the perfect, peaceful home. No, that stuff is for movies. Don't let the preacher's kids fool you either—no family is perfect!

However, at eighteen years old, that was still a future lesson. I was still desperately clinging to my mask, putting up the front that I was okay, that my life was normal, that I hadn't been exposed to the unspeakable as a child.

Somewhere along the passage of life between little girl and young adult, I had become lost. Being lost doesn't just apply to those who don't yet know Jesus; there are plenty of believers who are lost. Lost in tragedy, hurt, chronic pain, continual disappointment, rejection, abandonment, and grief—they all take a toll on the soul that onlookers may never see. I didn't know that I was lost, and it's not like anyone was looking for me. I wasn't even looking for me. But sure enough, a little of me was slipping away day by day.

Disappointment, rejection, loneliness, tragedy, unfulfilled dreams—life in general—had quietly formed layers over my heart while no one was watching. The quiet decay of my identity had started years before I even knew that it existed, but like a mold, it had spread, slowly infecting areas of my life, all the while disguising itself as normal.

The quiet decay of my identity had started years before.

I didn't like normal, but I wanted to feel it with every fiber of my being. Meanwhile, the preacher droned on with his never-ending, unintelligible commentary as the movie of my life played in my mind...

Far from Normal

I remember the day when I knew that my life was far from normal.

As I climbed up high in the branches on the lone tree at the far end of our Catholic school playground, I found my happy place. The green leaves were the perfect covering for this defiant action of tree climbing, while simultaneously providing me with a sense of achievement, knowing that I had the perfect vantage point from which to spot approaching trespassers or Nazi-trained lunch ladies. Either way, this was my space, my castle, and I was ready to defend it.

There were very few areas of my life that were under my control at five years of age, but tree climbing was definitely one of them. My legs dangling in the breeze, knees grazed and green from the grass, curly red pigtails askew, I watched the world go by. Safe.

Now, there was one girl in my class who intrigued me. Something about Lucy Castille drew me in. For a start, she always looked perfect, even at the end of the school day. Her uniform shirt was still tucked into her skirt, her whiter than white socks were never rolled down round her ankles like mine, and those blonde braids had not a strand out of place. She had it all going for her, and to top it off, I was her friend!

I loved going to play at Lucy's house. She had a big house in the posh part of town, and after dinner they always had dessert. Pink blancmange. It looked like Angel Delight to me, except it wasn't made from a packet, and it tasted like heaven.

The first time I went to play at Lucy's house, I didn't know they were religious. It never occurred to me that anyone was any different from my family. Turns out we were admitted into the school on account that my mum was a school lunch lady and, therefore, by-passed the religious requirements of admission.

The Castille's though, they were the real deal. Their whole family ate dinner together, and they said "grace" before they ate even a bite. I never figured out who Grace was, but they were insistent they had to pray to her first, and apparently, she preferred it if you didn't look when you did because we all had to close our eyes and bow our heads.

This was the first godly family I ever remember meeting. I saw something in them that I wanted. My heart ached for something I knew I was missing but had no words to describe.

From high in the perch of my tree, I watched Lucy spinning and twirling below me on the playground, with not a care in the world. That's when I realized my life was far from normal.

Lost Innocence

Despite our family's lack of structured religious upbringing, my parents instilled in my brother and I a strong sense of moral justice. We knew right from wrong; we knew it was wrong to steal and lie and cheat. We also knew that God created the world, that Heaven is where the good people go when they die, and that a little white lie that caused no harm, or enabled us to get a good deal, was okay by Him.

Like when we hid behind the sofa so the milk man would think we were out when we didn't have the right change to pay his bill. Or when I pretended to be younger than I actually was so we could buy a cheaper train ticket. These were "little white lies" that we thought never hurt anyone and made common sense according to worldly logic.

Then there were the other lies that I didn't know what to do with. The lies I told my parents to hide the truth, to hide the shame, to keep us safe…or so I thought.

Before I started school, I didn't think about it much. I didn't know what to think. A four-year-old sitting on her grandpa's lap to read a story would not be expecting a hand to slip down into her panties. I had no point of reference for that experience, no words to explain the way that it made me feel, no way to fill the void that just opened in my soul. He didn't say anything to me that first time. He just quietly stole my innocence.

The world became a smaller place with each revelation of what normal life should look like. As I watched my friend Lucy twirling the hula hoop below me, giggling as she spun with her braids spinning like a helicopter rotor, I wanted to be her. Just for a day, to forget everything and feel clean inside again.

As the days rolled by into years, the sometimes-daily violations inflicted on my little body grew more intense. I lost hope of it ending, and instead developed ways to cope, to control any areas of my life that I could. I concluded, after much thought on the subject, that if God created the heavens and the earth, Heaven sounded like a more promising proposition.

Relocating there would be the logical goal of my existence. One had to leave Earth to gain entry to Heaven, which would solve multiple issues. So, I began to plan my journey there and develop an exit strategy from this world.

I was too young to truly understand the concept of suicide, so that wasn't part of my plan. In the logic of an eight-year-old, purposefully shrinking myself would accomplish my goal. Shrinking from sight, shrinking inside myself, then later as a teen, shrinking through self-starvation, and praying that Grandpa wouldn't make me a teenage pregnancy statistic.

Interestingly, contemplating death was not a sad choice for me. I knew innately that God loved me, and I talked to Him daily. The longing to know God was in me from as early as I can remember. It didn't take too long to figure out that talking my feelings through with God was more beneficial than crying about them.

Crying never changed my situation. The pain was still there afterward, and the feelings of disgust, self-loathing and shame were just as real. But talking to God made me feel special, different for the right reason. Like I had a secret of the good kind, a friend to confide in.

ALL IS NOT LOST

Despite my ignorance of any religious instruction, other than morning mass at school, I had a relationship with Almighty God. I didn't know about sin, or salvation, or even that Jesus was anything more than a baby in a manger, but my God was real, and I was convinced that He was taking me to Heaven one day!

Talking my feelings through with God was more beneficial than crying about them.

For I am not ashamed of the gospel of Christ, for it is the power of God to salvation for everyone who believes, for the Jew first and also for the Greek.

Romans 1:16

Face to Face

Just as it was not God's plan for me to suffer at the hands of a man, it was not God's plan for me to end up in the ICU fighting for my life. It was not God who caused me to have the asthma attack that separated my spirit from my body at the age of twelve, but it *was* God who I met face to face that night in the middle of that mess.

I'd never heard of any out of body experiences or spoken to anyone who could describe Heaven to me. The only people I knew at twelve years old who had been to Heaven had become permanent residents, and they never called home! It would be decades later until I found out that there are others with experiences like mine.

The years of suppressing my emotions, to hide the pain of trauma, had chipped away at the childlike faith inside of me. Trauma does that. Lie after lie that become imbedded in a person's soul, eventually cause the heart to harden and become dull, spiritually insensitive.

So, by the time I was twelve, I didn't know if God was still there or if He still cared. And if He was and did then why didn't He make Grandpa stop? I had bought the lie too. God was God—all powerful—but the one lie that constantly whispered in my ear, *How can God love you since He let all these bad things happen,* had been germinating in my heart. I didn't know it then, but I needed more than the powerful God Almighty. I needed God, the good, good Father.

Laying there in the hospital bed, as some level of conscious thought returned, I realized that I was not dead. Based on the hustle and bustle of activity around me, that was obviously more than the doctors knew. I tried to move or speak to let them know I could hear them, but my limbs would not cooperate. Despite my most focused attempt to open my eyes, or twitch a finger, there was nothing I could do to communicate. They looked upon my body and saw the outward shell without hearing my silent screams.

But I needed more than the powerful God Almighty. I needed God, the good, good Father.

At some point, a doctor peeled back one of my eyelids to shine a flashlight into my eye. I was looking back at him, but it was like he couldn't see me. Irritated, he mumbled his discontentment under his breath, "Incompetent, wet-behind-the-ears doctors," and something about disturbing him at home in the middle of his dinner party.

As he looked into my eyes, I saw sadness in his. He flicked between my pupils with his flashlight and drew his silent conclusion. He had nothing more to offer me. He was as lost as I was, painfully aware of the fragility of life—my life—as it slipped away in front of him.

I retreated inside of my body like a turtle curling up inside its shell. Wondering how this weird experience was going to end, and if I would be trapped like a prisoner inside my own body forever, a panic began to swell like a wave within me.

If no one can hear me screaming how will this end? Will I be zipped up in a body bag and buried in the ground or shoved in an oven to be burned to ashes?

I began concentrating on calming myself down. *This is no time to panic, Carlie—it's not going to help*, I told myself as convincingly as I could.

Relaxation crept over my soul, a welcome relief.

God, where are You? I needed to know now more than ever.

And then it happened. I started floating up through my body, which was still tied to the hospital bed with IV tubes, and various monitors all alarming at once. I saw the doctor pressing the mask over my nose and mouth, felt his little finger pressing under my chin to secure the seal of the mask to my face. Rhythmically squeezing the bag trying to get me to breathe, thumping my chest so hard, my body bounced on the rigid bed with such vigor that I was sure my ribs would crack, shouting at each other, ripping open syringe packets to pump drugs into my veins and scurrying about.

Suddenly, every cell in by body was at peace, except now I had two bodies. One was in the bed and the other was me, the real me. Very aware that the real me was not the one who was lying on the bed, I tried to reconcile how I was moving. I was walking, I think, but not consciously. Floating may be a more accurate description.

Turning away from the hospital bed, on my right was a set of white double doors that shone with light through their frosted glass windows. I found myself moving toward them and then through them as they swung open to the long hallway on the other side.

Passing through the door and down the hall, the light became brighter. It reminded me of the warmth that penetrates your body when you lie in the sun on a hot summer day. It was so inviting, so overwhelmingly peaceful and loving. I was captivated by it, drawn toward the light by a love that words cannot adequately describe.

As I continued down the hallway, I found myself pulled to the side. There was some kind of scaffolding, which I thought was odd. I mean, surely there is not going to be construction in Heaven, right? As I looked more closely, I saw that the scaffolding covered a gate. It was *my* gate.

Suddenly aware that I was not alone, I turned around to face the presence behind me.

The light shone so brightly that I couldn't look at His face, only down at His feet. They were big feet, feet that had walked many miles. They were beautiful feet. The figure in front of me was so close that His white robes brushed against my knees and I felt His warm breath on my head, flooding every cell in my body and making my toes tingle.

The memories of the day had melted away to the point I was not even conscious of them. I was completely captivated in the moment. My flesh was entirely at peace in the presence of this stranger who was towering over me. If I had been back in my earthly body, I would have been afraid, intimidated, and looking for an exit to get away from His gaze.

Yet, somehow, I felt like I knew this person, like I had always known Him. I knew things without Him using words, without either of us speaking. Words are inadequate to describe the depth of love and peace I experienced while in His presence. I wanted to stay in that moment forever.

I felt like I knew this person, like I had always known Him.

My knees began to wobble under my robe. I wasn't wearing the hospital gown anymore. I had on a white robe. I could see my legs waver as all of my muscles relaxed, but just before the point at which I thought I might melt onto the floor, a finger touched my chin. He lifted my face until our gazes met. The brightness that shone from his skin was so intense that it was difficult to make out His facial features without squinting.

I didn't know His name, but I knew who He was, and I knew He knew me. Like, *really* knew me. He knew everything about me, He always had. He had always been there, right beside me, holding my heart in the palm of His hand.

Now I saw it. My tender heart at four years old was all the while being protected from the evils of this world by My Creator, My Father. Like asteroids hitting the outer atmosphere of the earth and burning up was every physical and emotional violation, every weapon sent to crush me. Though they tried with great force, they could never penetrate those hands to loosen His grip on me. I was His, and I wanted to stay with Him forever.

But my visit was premature, and I knew I had to go back to my earthly life. No sooner had that thought entered my mind than it was gone…

> *When you abide under the shadow of Shaddai, you are hidden in the strength of God Most High. He's the hope that holds me and the stronghold to shelter me, the only God for me, and my great confidence. He will rescue you from every hidden trap of the enemy, and he will protect you from false accusation and any deadly curse. His massive arms are wrapped around you, protecting you. You can run under his covering of majesty and hide. His arms of faithfulness are a shield keeping you from harm.*
>
> Psalm 91:1-4 TPT

Chapter Three

Making a Comeback

Everyone loves to see the underdog make a comeback and
win, don't they? Whether it is an unknown soccer team from
the lowest division winning the league, or a tiny country from
the back side of the globe grabbing gold at the Olympics, something about this warms the heart. That feeling of elation and
relief when an insurmountable obstacle has been overcome is
something we can all relate to.

The determination to overcome, the will to live, the desire
to succeed and press on, and the sheer stubbornness to prove
life wrong when it says you can't is in us all. Sometimes it's
a little deeper down in the pit than we would like, but we all
yearn for victory. Science may refer to this as the laws of nature
or natural selection, but humankind has something distinctly
different on its side that nature does not account for: faith. By
faith we overcome the world (1 John 5:4, Philippians 4:13).

Not only are there many stories in the Bible about the underdog making a comeback to ultimate victory, but my own life is
an example of a modern-day underdog. Surviving the physical

and emotional trauma of a decade of sexual abuse, and then coming back to life after death is a pretty cool comeback story.

After my trip to Heaven, life for me moved on. It does that, whether we are ready or not. Kind of like a game of hide and seek when it's time to go find everyone, "I'm coming, ready or not!"

However, something inside me was not ready to move on. Physically I had bounced back from my dance with death, but I was not the same. I had met God face-to-face. I knew that God had spared my life for a reason. It was not a mistake. I was not a mistake.

Setting my heart to find His, into my teenaged years, I journeyed down…let's just say some paths less travelled. In the midst of searching for God, I discovered some spirituality of the wrong kind. Spiritualism, or Christian Spiritualism as I was duped, turns out is not Christian at all but demonic.

Before I knew what was happening, I was in too deep to find my own way out. I knew that my life was in danger. I slept with heavy objects under my pillow at night due to paranoia and spoke with demons face-to-face. They knew me, too. My life felt destined to repeat itself, a never-ending cycle of near-death experiences punctuated with glimmers of hope—kind of like a soap opera with just enough comic relief to stop the viewers from changing the channel to something less depressing!

During this "spiritual awakening," I was sneaking peeks at the dusty family Bible that we had on the bookshelf at home. Tucked in tight on the shelf, behind the glass cabinet door, I had to climb up on a chair and turn the old brass key to unlock its treasure.

More like a family relic, it had a burgundy cover, thick gold-edged pages, and it smelled like moth balls. I was drawn to it, like it would call to me from the shelf when I was alone. I didn't understand the words that were written in it; it was almost like it was written in code. Yet something inside me was yearning to read it, even if I didn't understand its contents. I just knew it held the secret to why my life had been spared.

I knew the Bible held the secret to why my life had been spared.

Spiritualism held me in its grasp, but now I see that I was safe, even in the midst of that battle. As I was drawn to the Word, my heart was still being held in His hands.

However, daily life became a challenge. Constant fear caused adrenaline to pump through my body, feeling at any moment that death was imminent through the evil powers that surrounded and consistantly talked to me. The scratching nails of a demonic presence clawed at my skin from the inside out. I just wanted to be free from the torment.

Although by now my physical torment via abuse had somewhat been constrained by the very fact that I was a teenager and not as available as when I was as a child, the emotional and spiritual anguish seemed never ending. It was a dark pit, and I began to wonder if God was still there, and if He was, if He even cared about me. Listening too long to the voices in my soul, which told me I could never be free from them, I was so lost.

I had said in my heart that there was only One who could rescue me from the grip of the enemy. In my simple logic, I had watched enough movies to know that good is a stronger power than evil. I reasoned that suicide would not end the torment because even if I took my life, the devil would have won me. The battle for my life was about more than just me, it was for all those who would follow behind me. It was for the family that I had and for those I had yet to meet. If ever there was a God, then now would be a good time for Him to show up!

A Knock on the Door

And there it was: the knock on the door that changed everything.

Ding-dong!

From my attic room, I heard the front doorbell chime. My seventeen-year-old heart would have leapt clear out of my chest had my ribcage not been in the way. Somehow, I knew this unexpected, unknown, unwitting caller had my answer.

I raced down both flights of stairs stumbling down the steps like I was being chased and my life depended on getting to the bottom.

> He did know me, and I now knew His name: Jesus.

The blurred outline of the stranger was visible through the glass door: black shirt, black jeans...dog collar? As I opened the door, I realized it wasn't some gothic teenager, but a vicar. He stood there with a tract in hand and a speech ready to convince me into the kingdom. But I didn't have time for that.

Without saying a word or giving him time to get past his introduction, I snatched the leaflet from his hand and slammed the door shut in his face. Mine must have been the easiest doorstep conversion that vicar would ever experience!

Clutching that tract close to my chest, I raced back up to the bedroom with my precious cargo and shut the door. I *knew* the contents of this simple leaflet held the key to my freedom.

As I read this "Why Jesus?" pamphlet, it described the One I had met in Heaven—He *did* know me, and I now knew *His* name: Jesus.

I read through the prayer of salvation and threw myself on my knees, expecting angels to appear, trumpets to sound and maybe a lightning bolt. (Actually, I think the anticipation of the lightning bolt was why I closed my eyes so tightly.) But nothing.

Nothing physical anyway. But I felt the cloud lift: the oppression that had been laying like a heavy weight on my shoulders, as a yoke around my neck, was gone.

[The Father] has delivered and drawn us to Himself out of the control and the dominion of darkness and has transferred us into the kingdom of the Son of His love.

Colossians 1:13 AMPC

It was done! I knew that I was eternally safe—not that safety in this physical world was taken for granted. I had lived so long with fear for my physical safety that it was a weird kind of normal, but I knew that the battle for my soul was over. This was a far greater victory, and one which would set not only the course of my earthly life, but one that determined my eternal life.

The peace of God washed over me with such a tangible presence that I'm sure the noise of the angels rejoicing drowned out the screeches of the demonic realm as they gave their final death cry. I was wondering if the neighbors down the street could hear them rattling their chains in defeat! The devil is such a loser!

This was the first day of the rest of my life. The first day of my real life in Christ. I can't say it was all easy from then on, but that day I realized that all was *not* lost—it was just the beginning.

> *The thief comes only in order to steal and kill and destroy. I came that they may have and enjoy life, and have it in abundance (to the full, till it overflows).*

John 10:10 AMPC

All was not lost—it was just the beginning.

When life had consisted so long of fighting just to survive, finally living in a place of safety seemed pretty sweet, for a while at least. The enemy had been defeated, satan had lost his grip on my life, and Jesus had captured my heart once again.

When I became a follower of Jesus, I was not wholly prepared for the challenges that were ahead of me. Life up to that point had been a series of obstacles emotionally, physically, and spiritually. There were several Goliaths that I had learned to live with, which the Lord would show me needed to be slain. This process was not a comfortable one, and as He began to gently show me the parts of my heart which were broken, it felt more painful before it felt better. Today though, I can see that killing those giants was essential, and it has changed how I now approach life's challenges and disappointments.

Jesus didn't promise us that we would not face problems in this life—quite the opposite—but He gave us the solution to overcome them:

> *These things I have spoken to you, that in Me you may have peace. In the world you will have tribulation; but be of good cheer, I have overcome the world.*
>
> John 16:33

Jesus didn't promise us that we would not face problems in this life, but He gave us the solution to overcome them.

This came from a man who knew the enormity of the challenge ahead of Him. He knew of the persecution, the torture and torment, the pain that was to come when He said these words, but He was not focused on those things. He was looking to the victory that lay beyond His situation.

Jesus was viewing life from the other side of the cross. His perspective was one of eternity, looking past the temporary pain and seeing the victory which would come. We can learn from Jesus' attitude on the eve of His crucifixion that even when it seems like it is, all is not lost! There is still a way forward on your path to victory, no matter what trauma you may have experienced in the past.

The Significance of Jesus' Sacrifice

I had lived under the constant threat of death—physically, spiritually, and emotionally—because I hadn't known that there was an alternative. But everything changes when we receive Jesus. As believers, we have become completely new in our spirits, and as the king of Glory takes up residence in our hearts, we are sealed in a relationship with God that satan can never touch (2 Corinthians 5:17). We are not the same anymore. We are made righteous and truly holy regardless of what we have done in the past, or how far from God we have run (2 Corinthians 5:21). We are new creations, now a part of God's family.

Being a child of the King has benefits! We have not been left like orphaned children, alone in the world just trying to survive through life and hoping we make it until we get to Heaven.

God is not a negligent father. He has equipped us well for this earthly life with everything we will ever need to defeat a hungry bear, a roaring lion, the playground bully, the giant of sickness and poverty, or even that inner voice of inadequacy that says we'll never make it.

Jesus defeated satan for us on the cross so that, when we received Him at salvation as the Lord of our lives, the power of the enemy was broken. He no longer has any right to mess with us.

> *Giving thanks to the Father, Who has qualified and made us fit to share the portion which is the inheritance of the saints (God's holy people) in the Light. [The Father] has delivered and drawn us to Himself out of the control and the dominion of darkness and has transferred us into the kingdom of the Son of His love.*
>
> Colossians 1:12-13 AMPC

The greatest transfer to ever impact mankind was not when man stepped foot on the moon, the discovery of penicillin, the fall of Rome, or the invention of electricity. Sure, these were life-altering moments for generations to come but they pale into insignificance compared to the power shift that happened in the spiritual realm when Jesus died and rose from the dead. The least talked about event in today's world continues to irreversibly affect every man, woman, and child for all of eternity, whether they realize it or not.

Jesus wasn't just hanging out in the tomb for a few days waiting to emerge, prepping Himself for the original coming out party. He went down to the pit of hell and cleaned house. He isn't a savior who is unfamiliar with the pits we find ourselves in; He has pit experience! He wiped out the handwriting on the wall of accusations that were lodged against us before we were even born, and stripped satan of his power over us.

The least talked about event in today's world continues to irreversibly affect every man, woman, and child for all of eternity.

And you, being dead in your trespasses and the uncircumcision of your flesh, He has made alive together with Him, having forgiven you all trespasses, having wiped out the handwriting of requirements that was against us, which was contrary to us. And He has taken it out of the way, having nailed it to the cross. Having disarmed principalities and powers, He made a public spectacle of them, triumphing over them in it.

Colossians 2:13-15

When there were no more demonic creatures left standing, Jesus took the keys of hell itself, issued satan a one-way ticket to the lake of fire, and reminded him not to mess with His kids or he would have Him to deal with. He secured our victory over every scheme of the enemy and took us from victim to conqueror!

Yet amid all these things we are more than conquerors and gain a surpassing victory through Him Who loved us. For I am persuaded beyond doubt (am sure) that neither death nor life, nor angels nor principalities, nor things impending and threatening nor things to come, nor powers, Nor height nor depth, nor anything else in all creation will be able to separate us from the love of God which is in Christ Jesus our Lord.

Romans 8:37-39 AMPC

Had I known the significance of Jesus' resurrection when I received salvation, I would not have continued to live the defeated Christian life for so long.

I am the Gateway. To enter through me is to experience life, freedom, and satisfaction. A thief has only one thing in mind—he wants to steal, slaughter, and destroy. But I have come to give you everything in abundance, more than you expect—life in its fullness until you overflow!

John 10:9-10 TPT

Eat the Feast

Knowing that he is defeated, satan's last play, his counterattack, is to deceive believers into thinking God is somehow behind their troubles so they will never come to the realization of the power that Jesus has deposited in them. If we really believe that God is at work in us for a greater good, allowing awful situations to manifest in our lives, we will never resist them. Instead, we become powerless over our adversary through passivity and see ourselves as victims of circumstance rather than as the victorious in Christ.

Jesus has provided for us a banquet in the presence of our enemies, a feast, the original all you can eat buffet! When we fail to see and take part in all that He has laid out for us, it's like walking up to the banquet, bypassing the vast abundant provision, heading for the carrot sticks, taking one little bite, and saying, "Oh, no, that's all for me, thanks. I really don't deserve any more. And I'm not sure that it's your will, Lord, for me to eat."

That would be ridiculous. The feast is right there in front of us. It's no longer a case of, "If it's God's will." The food is already set out! His will was made up at the point of provision, and provision is there in abundance. Our deserving of it is irrelevant—it's already there.

If you saw your friend or family member nibbling at a single carrot stick, you would invite them to taste all the other foods. You would load up a plate and take it to them, poke them with a chicken wing, or nudge them with a rib. You wouldn't leave them alone until they understood that the entire feast was for them, the price paid, in their honor.

Yet so many believers do this every day when they settle for barely surviving in life. Jesus came to give us a life that is full of vitality, vigorous abundance, more than enough, a life that is overflowing in victory!

Moving from the bottom of the pit to your path to victory begins and ends with Jesus, but it starts in our hearts. It is in the place where self-pity dies and the desire to really live is born. Victory and peace are not handed down to those in the pit but are found by those who look up and take the hand of the One who is reaching out to them.

Victory and peace are found by those who look up and take the hand of the One who is reaching out to them.

Chapter Four

A Step in the Right Direction

As I sat there in that church pew, reviewing the moving picture of my life, I acknowledged that my first year since being officially "saved" had not been typical one, if there is such a thing. Just a few months earlier, I wouldn't have been sitting on a pew in church but in a wheelchair, with very little feeling or control from my waist down.

The epileptic seizures I started having shortly after being born again had affected my brain to such a degree that I could no longer walk or control any of the muscles in my lower extremities. At eighteen years old, no one wants to hear, "You may never walk again; get used to your new life."

Something inside of me just screamed, *NO!* There were places in the world I knew that God was showing me I would go, things I had yet to accomplish, and a wheelchair was *not* part of those pictures. I didn't know very much about faith, but I knew enough to be dangerous to the devil.

I didn't know very much about faith, but I knew enough to be dangerous to the devil.

Not even knowing half of what I know now, I had been writing out scriptures and sticking them to my bedroom walls. I sat at home one day, meditating on a vision that I had of me doing something that seemed impossible at the time: climbing a mountain. No sooner had I begun to dwell on this than I received a notice of an upcoming trip to the Lake District with my church youth group. All kinds of outdoor activities were planned, including climbing, and I planned to be a part of them.

Everyone thought I was crazy, but I knew that wheelchair was never going to be permanent. It was not a part of who I was. Despite the prognosis, it did not define me. Looking back, I see now how hugely important this was. While being measured and fitted for a custom chair, I tried to tell the technician that it wasn't necessary, as I would be walking soon. They didn't get it.

But I dreamt about climbing that mountain. I imagined myself scrambling over boulders, pulling myself up on ropes and traversing narrow rock ledges. And then one day I had a thought. *I need to speak to my legs.* At this point, I was wondering about my sanity as well, but it just felt right.

I waited until everyone was out of the house and began to tell my body what it was going to do.

"Legs, you are strong! You bear weight." Pushing down on the arms of my wheelchair, I forced myself up into a standing position and one by one raised my hands. Seeing that my legs had obeyed my words thus far, I spoke again, "Foot, move!"

Every time I spoke, and then tried to move something that I previously couldn't, it moved! Each tiny step forward was followed by my own personal moment of celebration until I finally found myself ten feet away from the wheelchair, standing by the front door of our house. It was then I remembered that some youth were a couple of miles away playing tennis at the community court.

I had a choice to make. I could step out my front door and walk to the community court to play tennis with my friends. I figured, *why not?* I couldn't walk at all ten minutes earlier, and what was the alternative? Going back and sitting in the wheelchair? No, thank you.

So, I stepped out the door and began to walk, one step at a time. The look on their faces when I staggered up was priceless! It wasn't my best game of tennis, but it was a far cry more than what I had been able to accomplish that morning.

A few months later, I climbed the mountain I had been dreaming about. After that, I began to question the phrase *you can't* if it ever popped up in my mind. I had quite literally taken a step in the right direction!

The Comforter

So, sitting on a church pew was something to be thankful for, even if it was making my butt cheeks go to sleep. It certainly beat spending my life in a wheelchair! The church didn't really understand what had happened to me, and couldn't explain it, so we all just kind of moved on, like, "Yep, that was weird, but nothing to see here!"

In churches like mine, when you experience something without understanding it, the victory becomes an anomaly when it should be a normality. It's explained by, "Well, the Lord works in mysterious ways. You never know what He's going to do!" At least by then I knew beyond doubt that God *could* heal, if it was His will.

That issue of God's will: it plagued my relationship with Him. I felt like I was playing spiritual roulette every time I prayed. *Will He answer? Will He not?* Gradually, this devolved into, *Does He love me? Does He not?*

And that's what made me mad at God. I had known Him so closely when I was little. I'd felt Him touch my face in Heaven, I'd had a powerful salvation experience and had seen His healing power run through my body. Yet, I felt so alone, still so broken. Through abuse and physical challenges, I felt robbed of a childhood that was so lost it could never be found again.

I felt so alone, completely and utterly, earth-shatteringly alone in a pit of emotion so deep that I had no words to communicate it. I had spent so much time in my own mental prison, switched off every emotion that I could to protect myself, stuffed each negative thought carefully into the deepest crevasses of my brain, until not even I could find my way out to feel again. The pit of unworthiness was deep and dark and familiar.

What's the point? I thought. My life was on a trajectory of hurt, like a rollercoaster that never seemed to end, and I just wanted it to stop. I didn't understand the church language, I wasn't raised in church. I needed to know that the Jesus I once met face to face was still present.

Where was He in all of the mess? And fake church, with its perfect families and sermons with words I couldn't understand just made me angrier. There was one scripture that especially got under my skin. It *really* irritated me because I couldn't see how it worked:

> *And we know that all things work together for good to those who love God, to those who are the called according to His purpose.*
>
> Romans 8:28

Whenever I would hear this verse, familiar questions from my childhood rose up: *How could what happened to me possibly be good? Did God allow it? If He really loved me, why hadn't He stopped what was happening to me?*

This scripture is one of the most abused verses in the Bible and yet one of the most powerful. So often it is used to assume that if bad things are happening to us, that God must be orchestrating them for some greater good which we cannot see but must blindly believe.

However, what the devil intends for destruction, God really *can* turn around for our good. That doesn't mean that God is by default the author of tragedy, the formulator of trauma in our lives, or that somehow He is sending bad things our way to teach us a greater lesson. **God is not a child abuser!**

If I could travel back in time and talk to my teenage self, I would tell her to read the verses just prior to the one which brought so much hurt and confusion:

> *Likewise the Spirit also helpeth our infirmities: for we know not what we should pray for as we ought: but the Spirit itself maketh intercession for us with groanings which cannot be uttered. And he that searcheth the hearts knoweth what is the mind of the Spirit, because he maketh intercession for the saints according to the will of God.*

> Romans 8:26-27 KJV

God is far from tormenting us with tragedy; He doesn't use narcissistic teaching methods. In fact, knowing that in this life we would face troubles (John 16:33), He sent us the Holy Spirit to help us in these times when it seems like all is lost.

The Holy Spirit has several roles, but one of them is our helper, our comforter. This word *helpeth* is a complex word in the Greek, *sunantilambanomai*. It denotes a partnership, a coming alongside someone to assist them in a challenge, to remove the hinderance and return to them what belongs to them. Literally to take hold of the problem with us, to stand with us in the midst of our infirmities or weakness.

The word *infirmities* is translated from the Greek *astheneia*, which describes people who are sick or broken in their bodies, minds, or emotions. This doesn't sound like a God who is distant, harsh, or uncaring. No, He cares so much for us that He sent His Holy Spirit on a rescue mission to the pit of our despair.

The Holy Spirit intercedes for us. Intercession is a powerful force. The word for *intercession* here in Romans 8:26 is only found once in the Bible. The Greek is *huperentugchanó* and describes a person falling into a pit on behalf of another in order to rescue him and pull him out. When we don't know how to pray, when we are at the end of our rope, in the worst condition possible physically, emotionally, spiritually, we can pray in the Spirit and **boom**! The Holy Spirit enters the equation and puts the odds in our favor as He comes alongside us, takes hold of the challenge for us, forces it out of the way, secures our harness and hoists us up out of that pit!

My 18-year-old self would have benefited greatly from this understanding!

Just like me, there are many hurting Christians in the world today who have believed the lie that God is working a greater purpose in us by allowing tragedy and destruction in our lives, things from which He has the power to protect us, or even prevent them entirely. This is not scriptural, no matter how much it is repeated. God is good, and only good, and He doesn't package up pain and call it good.

> *Do not be misled, my beloved brethren. Every good gift and every perfect (free, large, full) gift is from above; it comes down from the Father of all [that gives] light, in [the shining of] Whom there can be no variation [rising or setting] or shadow cast by His turning [as in an eclipse].*
>
> James 1:16-17 AMPC

God is good, and only good, and He doesn't package up pain and call it good.

Romans 8:27-28 angered me so much because I approached it as a victim. I didn't know what the will of God was for me. I only saw the bad and attributed it to God. However, the will of

God isn't mysterious or hidden. Right here in James, God's will is made perfectly clear: He gives us good and perfect gifts, and He is only light, never darkness!

When the Spirit makes intercession for you according to the will of God, it is always for your good: for healing, for life abundantly, for protection and deliverance, for provision. We sometimes struggle to receive these things because we cannot imagine a God who is so good, or so for us, who knows all of our faults and loves us anyway.

The Way Out

The movie in my mind was coming to an end, and there I sat on the pew, the preacher still monologuing his dissertation on the seven candlesticks of Revelation. My life, all eighteen years had flashed before me, and I think he was still on the same verse.

I wasn't prepared for what happened next.

The voice thundered around the room. It reverberated through every cell in my body and blew the hair across the vicar's head. It was a mighty rushing wind, like the sound of many waters. Power surged, lights flickered, and I'm pretty sure my heart stopped momentarily.

Nobody moved. It was like time froze. They had said Jesus was coming soon, and my bet was that it was happening right then! Just as I looked around, expecting to see angels, or people in the congregation being sucked up through the roof into Heaven, I heard God's audible voice:

I know you, and I love you.

It was as if each word was a thousand words, they pierced so deeply into my soul. Every pain, every traumatic encounter, every moment of neglect, every lie I had believed, every insecurity I had harbored, every negative opinion of others that had rooted itself in my heart—all were wiped away. I knew that He had been there with me through it all, holding my heart and shielding me from destruction.

"I know you, and I love you." – God

God loved me. Not just liked me—and not because He had to—but *really* loved me. As that love washed over me, suddenly I didn't care about my scars. What can man do to me, when my Father loves me? I realized that He knows us so intimately and protects us from things we don't even know are there.

The destruction I had felt moments before hadn't—couldn't—come from Him, but I had been holding on to it. In that moment, I let it all go, like it didn't belong to my life anymore. The love of God flooded the dark, wounded places of my heart until there were none left.

One word from God changed everything. It contained all the power I'd ever need to live a life of victory.

As I looked around, no one else appeared to have heard Him. Others may have been unaffected, but it profoundly touched my life. I ran home from church that night a changed woman. I felt like I could face any skeleton in the closet, any giant in the battle, and know confidently that I was more than a conqueror.

Forgiving the Unforgivable

The next morning our doorbell rang. It was Grandpa.

Without flinching, the love of God shot through me. I flung my arms around the neck of the man who had tormented and abused me for a decade. Forgiveness had never felt so good!

So often, emotional healing gets overlooked, but the hidden scars, the ones other people cannot see, cause the deepest wounds.

Forgiveness is essential, but impossible without first receiving the love of God. We love because He first loved us (1 John 4:19). My journey of forgiveness began that day. It was a moment of realization that everything that hurts in this life will—one day—not matter. We are built for an eternal destination, by a Creator who loves and equips us to thrive, even while on assignment in this dark and temporary world.

Our bodies decay: from the moment we are born, we are on the clock. Never in my life have I seen a greater acceleration of this decay than during the years that I held on to *my* pain. I had created the victim within me, not Grandpa. He was just the tool the devil used to get me on the path of self-destruction.

Forgiveness is essential, but impossible without first receiving the love of God.

Bad things happen to good people. They become victims of circumstance. But when those circumstances have changed, yet the person remains a victim, it is because the "victim" has gotten inside of them.

The road of forgiveness is long, and fraught with opportunities to veer off course. No one said that it would easy, but I am convinced that there is no other option for those who have become lost if they want to find their way again. A heart which holds onto to hatred, offense and unforgiveness is a heart without peace.

Ultimately, when we hang onto these thoughts, continually meditating on those people or events that caused pain, we begin to dig deeper down into the pit where they had put us, rather than allowing the Holy spirit to rescue us out of it. It's like drinking poison while hoping the other person is affected by it.

When we hold on to offense and unforgiveness, we are subconsciously saying, "Jesus may have forgiven your sin on the cross, but I'm going to hold onto it." We are behaving as though

Jesus' sacrifice wasn't enough to cover the pain, trauma, and memories that someone or something has left with us.

My journey had some twists and turns in it. There were days when I had to daily pray for those who hurt me. I had to make the decision to only speak over them blessing rather than curses. I didn't yet know how to pray, so I had to allow the Holy Spirit to help me pray as I ought.

One thing the Lord did was show me a vision of how Grandpa looked as an infant, before he grew up into a monster. I saw him as a child, perfectly created by a God who loves him. He helped me to see Grandpa separately from his sin, to see the plans and the life He had planned for him before he chose sin. Who I saw was just another broken, hurting child. Hurting people hurt people. I found compassion for him that he didn't deserve. Isn't that what God shows to us every day?

There is a release that happens when we verbally shout it out, physically releasing all of the pain and hurt that has been bottled up inside. This is why people literally lash out at others—they are finding a release for emotional pain through a physical action. While destructive when used incorrectly, allowing a physical release of emotional pain—like screaming into a pillow, or hitting a punching bag—is healthy.

There are many different constructive ways to let go of bottled up unforgiveness, anger and other negative emotions, which don't require a physical release. Some people find it helpful to write a breakup letter. It might go something like this:

____(name)____. I'm writing this to you today to let you know that this will be the last time we communicate. I refuse to listen to or be moved by your lies anymore. I release every negative thought and feeling I associate with you. You are not a part of who I am. You have no authority in my life and no power over me.

I invite the Holy Spirit to help me in directing my thoughts toward love and forgiveness every time you come to mind. I surrender my emotions to the Lord. Now you, _____, are the Lord's problem to deal with. Jesus's blood has paid for my sin and yours. I have no right hold you accountable through unforgiveness in my heart. I repent of holding on to toxic unforgiveness, and I accept His healing power into my heart, in Jesus' name.

When seeking after healing for illness in your physical body, emotional healing often precedes physical healing. It is real, and there is real healing for your heart.

But He was wounded for our transgressions, He was bruised for our iniquities; The chastisement for our peace was upon Him, And by His stripes we are healed.

Isaiah 53:5

He restores my soul…

Psalm 23:3

For as he thinks in his heart, so is he…

Proverbs 23:7

Chapter Five

Changing Identity

It's obvious that I received miraculous healing from God by the time I was eighteen. I was physically raised from death after a fatal asthma attack, healed from paralysis caused by repeated epileptic seizures, *and* emotionally healed from sexual abuse and the associated unforgiveness. However, those were only stepping-stones on my path from trauma to victory.

I was still an epileptic.

Over the years, many people have asked some form of these questions: "You got out of a wheelchair as a teenager! How did you not understand that healing was God's will? Why weren't you completely healed of epilepsy at the same time?"

Living life abundantly in the fullness of all Jesus paid for often requires a change of identity, in how we see ourselves and in how we think. The longer we have lived a particular way, the more ingrained it becomes in our minds as normal. Abuse was a device of the enemy that made me feel worthless. Sickness was a lie of the enemy that had plagued me since birth, and together they caused me to see myself as a sick person, as a victim.

The longer we have lived a particular way, the more ingrained it becomes in our minds as normal.

Before I received Christ, I was sick to the point of death many times, and nothing changed in that realm after I was saved. Jesus had done His part. The issue was not with God, it was me. I was just as sick in my thinking as I was in my body because sickness had become a part of my identity.

I was the one standing at the banquet eating the carrot stick because I didn't know that God wasn't the author of my sickness. So, yes, I got up out of my wheelchair and walked, but I thought sometimes God heals, and sometimes He doesn't. My church couldn't really explain it, so it was accounted as one of those "mysterious ways" of God.

You can't fight what you embrace, so if it wasn't asthma, it was epilepsy, and we were doing life together. I had been sick so long, I just didn't really know any differently. It was just part of who I was. "Carlie, the epileptic." I guess I must have missed Luke 5 in my Bible!

And it happened when He was in a certain city, that behold, a man who was full of leprosy saw Jesus; and

he fell on his face and implored Him, saying, "Lord, if
You are willing, You can make me clean." Then He put
out His hand and touched him, saying, "I am willing;
be cleansed." Immediately the leprosy left him.

Luke 5:12-13

Dealing with sickness my entire life, the standard response I received from elders in the faith was, "You never can know the will or mind of God. His ways are higher than our ways." This explanation was churned out following every episode of tragedy, confusion, hardship, sickness, roadblock, and even the unexplainable good, like when my paralysis was healed. It seemed God received credit for as much evil as He did good. I loved God with all my heart but could not understand how, if He was so loving, it could be His plan for us to suffer in so many ways.

Yet, as I moved into adulthood, every time I read the New Testament, I saw that it was full of examples of healings and miracles. I searched the Bible for an expiration date to these manifestations but found none.

In the gospels, we see that every person who approached Jesus for healing was fully restored. Jesus was always willing to help them. If God's will is for us to be sick, Jesus wouldn't have gone about *"doing good and healing all who were oppressed by the devil"* (Acts 10:38). It was the *devil* who was doing the oppressing, not God.

If healing wasn't always God's will, He wouldn't have provided it as part of the atonement with salvation, deliverance, and prosperity.

Beloved, I wish above all things that thou mayest prosper and be in health, even as thy soul prospereth.

3 John 2 KJV

My simple logic told me that if this same power was indeed at work in me now like it was in Jesus, then I should be seeing healings and miracles like Jesus did (Romans 8:11). Perhaps all I'd been taught was wrong. Maybe my thinking was wrong. It comforted me to know that if something was wrong on my end, in my thinking, I could change me!

A Change of Heart

Years later, I was married and a mum of three small children. I began frequenting a midday women's Bible study. This small group of ladies belonged to a different church than the one I attended, but I was drawn to them. As young mothers with a passion for God, these ladies weren't afraid to show their zeal. They believed in speaking in tongues, but I noticed they did not exude a fake spirituality. They spoke like the people in the Bible. They talked to God like a friend. And the most intriguing thing for me was that God talked back!

These ladies had something I did not, and I wanted it! They soon became my close friends and demonstrated Jesus to me in a way I had never experienced. The Holy Spirit was a strange and mysterious concept to me, yet this group provided a safe place in which the gifts of the Spirit could operate. It was here that I first heard God speak to me.

One particularly memorable day, we were practicing listening to the voice of God. I sat as still as I could, cleared my mind of wandering thoughts, and listened. To my surprise, thoughts began to pop into my head which seemed to come from nowhere. Realizing that these thoughts were so foreign they couldn't be me, and that none of the other ladies were trying to whisper in my ear, I realized it was the Lord speaking to me!

At this point in my life, I had *never* seen or heard of anyone receiving healing in a supernatural way after receiving prayer. Certainly, as a teenager I had been healed when I walked out of my wheelchair, but no one had actually prayed for me. I hadn't even really prayed for myself!

I knew of people who thanked God for healing them, and I am sure that He had a part to play in it, but they all followed some course of medical treatment. Rather than seeing this as a matter of divine intervention, the nurse part of me had concluded that medicine had done its job.

In my experience, Christians prayed for the sick more from duty than with any real expectancy. We always ended our prayers with, "If it be Thy will, Lord," and that hardly seemed a guarantee. But how could we know if God was in a good mood? Or if the person being prayed for deserved healing? Or even if God still healed?

As I sat in that Bible study, listening to the Lord and processing the thoughts He was bringing to my mind, one of them was of James 5:14-15:

Is anyone among you sick? Let him call for the elders of the church, and let them pray over him, anointing him with oil in the name of the Lord. And the prayer of faith will save the sick, and the Lord will raise him up. And if he has committed sins, he will be forgiven.

I realized that it wasn't just any prayer that "saved the sick." Healing required a prayer of *faith*. I thought, *Well, if faith is to be sure of the things I hope for and certain of the things I cannot see* (Hebrews 11:1), *then praying with faith involves a level of **certainty**, not wonder.*

Apparently, when James prayed for the sick, he was not *asking* God to heal them, but was *expecting* to see them healed. No wonder I hadn't seen or heard of any healings! There was clearly no shortage of sick or praying people, but there was a shortage of faith.

I realized that faith has to be present for healing to be received.

As I continued pondering these things, I heard something that sounded so alien to me I knew it could never have come from my flesh. I could never have come up with it on my own.

Carlie, you have held Me outside of the epilepsy. You don't need to. I want to take it from you if you want me to. In two weeks' time, you can be free from this if you choose to be. Flip the switch.

In my mind, I saw a light switch. I knew that if I flipped the switch, the epilepsy I had struggled with since childhood would be gone.

Faith has to be present for healing to be received.

The profoundness of this statement hit me like a freight train. If I had been talking, I would have become speechless. Seconds before God spoke, I had been a sufferer, a victim of life and circumstance just trying to survive. Now I understood that the God of the universe had put the power to "choose life" in my hands.

A hundred questions raced through my head. *Could it really be that simple? Do I really have a choice to change my circumstances? Can my thoughts and beliefs really change my physical condition?*

According to Scripture, we do have a choice to make. Life is not automatic. God's perfect will doesn't happen by accident. We have to choose God's blessing over the devil's curse.

I call heaven and earth as witnesses today against you, that I have set before you life and death, blessing and cursing; therefore **choose life,** *that both you and your descendants may live.*

Deuteronomy 30:19
(emphasis added)

Life is meant to be a blessing but receiving that blessing starts with a choice—our choice.

God put the choice to live before me. Looking around at the other ladies in the study group, I could see others opening their eyes, and I knew it was time to go. Fearing I had lost my mind, and that the others could see it, I said nothing. I knew I would have a lot to think about during the next two weeks.

Dirty Little Secrets Revealed

I continued to keep the afternoon's events to myself—I didn't even share what had happened with my husband. I was certain the account would sound as ridiculous to him as it did to me. I decided that if what I'd experienced really was God speaking, and not some strange side effect from one of the dozen or so medications I ingested daily, then I wanted Him to show me it was real.

My brain tried very hard to convince me that I had just imagined the whole incident, but I knew it was of God. And one surprising consequence I had not anticipated was that every time I searched my heart, I found that the thought of being healed filled me with dread.

I know it sounds silly, but I was afraid of being healed. All my life I had been sick in some way. I hated to admit it, but a part of me needed to be sick. It had become a way of life, a part of my identity, an excuse when I needed something to hide behind. It made me special. I was ashamed and embarrassed at my own neediness, but I didn't know how to be well. However, I knew my flesh hadn't dreamt up the notion of being healed!

I barely noticed as two weeks ticked by. I was too busy thinking about all the ways I had adapted my daily life around the disease of epilepsy. I began to notice the small details of my life: the drug routine, the hospital appointments and admissions, the babysitter who came to sit for me because I could not be left alone with my children.

I noticed the locks we installed at the top of each door so I could contain the toddlers in a safe place when I felt a seizure coming. I remembered the number of times I had awoken in a strange hospital room wondering who I was and where the twigs in my hair had come from. I remembered meeting my baby girl for the first time and thinking, *How do I know that she is mine?* (I was mid-seizure and unconscious during her delivery.)

I came to realize that not being able to work, drive or simply function independently as a healthy adult had messed with my thinking. Epilepsy had slowly taken over larger and larger pieces of my life. It dictated how I spent my time, where I could go, and those with whom I could associate. It told me how to plan my day, what to eat and when to sleep. It separated me from my family and strained my relationships. Epilepsy had caused financial hardships and dictated my future.

But worse than all of these things, it was sucking away my confidence and self-worth like a disgusting parasite. Epilepsy was a different kind of abuser than my grandfather had been, but it was just as effective at creating another kind of victim.

And yet, the thought of being normal and healthy terrified me. I had no track record of health. It was foreign ground to me. Epilepsy had given me a crutch, a way out when I didn't want to do something. If I was normal, I could work a job and drive a car. That was the bottom of the barrel, an ugly truth in my heart that I didn't even know was there. Epilepsy made me feel special.

Once all these dirty little secrets surfaced within me, I just could not squeeze them all back inside. Now that I knew they were there, I couldn't unknow them, and I didn't really want to. My heart was changing. Ever so gently, the Holy Spirit was convicting me of the dark insecurities of my heart so He could show me my salvation.

The thief does not come except to steal, and to kill, and to destroy. I have come that they may have life, and that they may have it more abundantly.

John 10:10

A Changed Imagination

This verse revolutionized my thought life. For the first time, with the Holy Spirit's help, I saw that the enemy came to kill, steal, and destroy me physically, emotionally, and spiritually. But Jesus came to give me life and show me how to live it. Even though it was uncomfortable for a while, the Holy Spirit guided me into truth so He could bring healing, peace, love, joy, and freedom to my life (John 16:13).

I began to consider what life would be like without epilepsy. I thought of what it would be like to plan and follow my dreams, to have enough energy for the day, to walk down the stairs and know that I would make it to the bottom without having a seizure.

I dreamed of what life would look like if I no longer fell asleep without warning or rocked myself into a fetal position when the side effects of my disease cramped my muscles. I thought of how it would be to walk alone, to drive, to explore, to not have to explain this condition or take medication or stay in the hospital or even go to the doctor anymore. My dream was huge!

But even bigger than my dream of life without epilepsy was the miracle that no one ever saw. The biggest part of my healing was the revelation that **I was special simply because I had become a child of God**. I didn't need to be afraid; God was with me. He would always be my hiding place.

He who dwells in the secret place of the Most High shall abide under the shadow of the Almighty. I will say of the Lord, "He is my refuge and my fortress; my God, in Him I will trust." Surely He shall deliver you from the snare of the fowler and from the perilous pestilence... "With long life I will satisfy him, and show him My salvation."

Psalm 91:1-3, 16

This passage showed me that if put my trust in the Lord, He would deliver me from epilepsy. I was finally ready to give the disease that had taken over my life to the Lord. I knew I was no longer powerless in this situation. I knew it was my decision to accept or reject the gift God had for me, and I knew my decision would determine whether or not I continued to allow the enemy to steal from my life. I was ready. I knew that the moment I flipped the switch in my mind, epilepsy would be gone.

The Flip of a Switch

Being rather preoccupied, I had forgotten that two weeks was the timeframe God had given me in prayer. On the way to my women's Bible study that Friday, I wondered if everything that I had heard, felt, and experienced of God had really happened. I had never heard of anyone talking with God like I had. I'd never heard of anyone being healed, had never seen anyone be healed. What if I was crazy?

It was probably heresy; I was going to die, struck by lightning for stupidity or blasphemy. Well, at least I hadn't spoken out my thoughts or told anyone... But what if it really was God? I decided to test the matter. If it really had been God speaking to me, then someone would offer to pray for me at Bible study. If no one offered to pray for me, then I would chalk the whole thing up to my imagination and would forget about it all.

The ladies gathered as usual with the little kids playing in the hallway, quietly dismantling the house. Occasionally the conversation broke to allow a mom to apply an ice pack to newly slapped skin or attend to a pungent bottom, but nothing out of the ordinary happened, and suddenly it was time to go. Rounding up my tribe and heading for the front door, one of the ladies stopped and turned toward me. "I need to pray for you," she said.

I don't remember what she prayed. I know it was quick, a micro prayer that didn't add an "if it be Thy will" to its end. Immediately, I felt heat throughout my body, and in my mind, I flipped the switch of epilepsy off. Nothing on the outside of me changed, but I knew it was done.

> Nothing on the outside of me changed, but I knew it was done.

Immediately, my life changed from having multiple seizures a day to having zero, and I've never had another seizure since!

I gained a new identity and it resulted in my physical healing. I am no longer Carlie the epileptic, I am Carlie the healed of the Lord!

In the same way, regardless of the giants you may be facing in your life, you can also make a comeback. Like I did, you may see yourself as a victim, as weak, or ill-equipped to fight your giants. But there is a version of you that has been hidden. It is time to identify with who you really are. You are a child of the Most High God and fully equipped to emerge victorious!

Chapter Six

Discovering Your New Identity

Up until my healing from epilepsy, my identity had been that of a victim. Until the Lord lovingly showed me the truth, I didn't see myself as a champion. My personal path from trauma to victory began with a change in my perspective. Rather than seeing myself as a victim, I had to discover my new identity as a victorious, overcoming, beloved child of God! Your path to victory may not be identical to mine, but discovering your true identity is a vital stepping-stone for us all.

As an heir to the throne of England, Prince George was born into the royal household. He did nothing himself to deserve such opportunity, or favor. The benefits he enjoys while growing up are based on his birthright, not on his performance. Yet, as a member of the royal family, he is being raised differently. It isn't only because he lives in splendor, but it will affect the way he thinks. He will be raised with the knowledge of who he is. He will learn that he has a defined purpose, that he is a leader, and as such it will influence his choices: the relationships he engages in, the career path he pursues, etc. His lifestyle will reflect his calling and identity.

But you are a chosen generation, a royal priesthood, a holy nation, His own special people, that you may proclaim the praises of Him who called you out of darkness into His marvelous light.

1 Peter 2:9

We may not have all been naturally born into a life of earthly privilege, but we have all been born-again into a royal family. We have been adopted into the family of God (Ephesians 1:5), chosen by Him, and set apart for great things (John 15:16).

We have been adopted into the family of God.

As God's children, we have been given a new identity. Like a natural prince or princess, this is nothing that we earn, but it comes with all the benefits of a royal birthright: favor (Luke 2:52, Romans 8:17), provision (Psalm 34:10), protection (Mark 16:18, Psalm 91), and purpose (Ephesians 2:10)!

The challenge comes when we look around us, and our situation doesn't match up with what we believe. When we have accepted the truth of our identity, yet our natural circumstances still reflect humble beginnings. It is easy to become discouraged and start agreeing with the world's view of us, rather than God's. However, the Word of God is full of examples of people who were zeros in the eyes of the world but who God called heroes!

For example, King David had to navigate many situations where the world around him didn't match up to the word God had given him. When Samuel the prophet anointed David as king, he was the least likely of all his brothers to amount to much. David was the youngest, so he was not even invited to the king-picking party—they had to go get him in from the sheep field! It must have been an awkward moment. Samuel even made them all remain standing while they waited on David's arrival (1 Samuel 16-17)!

Yet, David—the youngest, most humble of all his brothers—was anointed king. What happened next was not a gold chariot, silk robe or royal feast. No, he went back out to look after the sheep! That's right, he smelled like sheep. It took a while before anything in the natural changed.

Meanwhile, David knew in his heart that God had set him apart for great things and was with him. He spent his early years writing songs of praise and worship to the Lord. He practiced his skills with his slingshot, and God gave him the strength to kill natural predators that came after his flock. Although the anointed King of Israel, he simply continued to grow and develop in his relationship with God.

It was this identity and confidence in his relationship with the Lord that produced the boldness he needed to defeat Goliath! In the face of that adversity, David killed Goliath first in his thinking as he saw himself as the victorious king that he was appointed to be. He walked in his authority against that giant, not because he was a soldier in the natural, but because he knew his true identity in his relationship with God.

In the same way, knowing your true identity as a child of God is the first step in embracing the truth that, even as an underdog, you are created to make a comeback to victory!

Knowing your true identity as a child of God is the first step in making your comeback to victory!

The Rights of Identity

In the story of the Prodigal Son, in Luke 15:20-32, the son took his inheritance, irresponsibly spent it all, and ended up starving, feeding pigs for a living. He then realized that at least his father would ensure he would have a roof over his head, and three square meals a day, so he went back home.

The prodigal son thought he would be returning home in shame, as a failure, but his father actually ran to him with joy! The father restored his son's identity with the finest robe. He also restored his authority, as his father's representative, with a family ring. The son had not earned these things in any way. In fact, with all he had done, he deserved to be treated like a servant! Yet, his behavior was not an indicator of his identity. His sonship is what determined his rights and authority.

An interesting aspect of this story to note is the attitude of the other son. Although his behavior had been respectful, responsible, and good, he didn't understand his true identity as a son either. In his mind, he had replaced good behavior as the definition of his identity, rather than his relationship with his father. Therefore, when his irresponsible brother returned and was blessed, he responded with insecurity and jealousy.

If our identity is not in God, it will be in something else—work, money, position, power, performance, popularity, sickness, family, etc. None of these can bring peace or happiness but will cause instability in receiving from God.

Having an incorrect concept of our identity results in insecurity, which hinders faith. It looks for approval from others rather than from God and is easily swayed by the opinions of man. This kind of identity is based on our own performance. It is self-righteous and self-centered. If our faith is based on these things, it will be as weak and double-minded as the flesh upon which it is based.

The only way to truly have faith is when the will of God is known. Knowing your true identity as a child of God, with the rights and authority that comes with that relationship, will allow you to stand strong in faith to receive every good thing God has for you.

Stand in Your Identity

God has promised so many good things to His children. The Gospel is truly good news! However, we will only see these things come to pass in our lives when we *believe* them. And the confident faith that is required for receiving God's promises begins with knowing our true identity as beloved children of God.

When you look at yourself in the natural, you will pick out every fault and flaw. You will see every reason why you are *not* qualified to receive good things from God. However, when God sees you, He sees His born-again, righteous child. His Spirit dwells in you, and when He sees you, He sees Jesus!

In order to stand strong in your identity, you must begin to see yourself the way God sees you. He doesn't see your daily mistakes. He doesn't look at you based on your outward behavior or appearance. He perceives your true identity according to your spirit. And your spirit is brand-new, perfect, righteous, and truly holy!

...For the Lord does not see as man sees; for man looks at the outward appearance, but the Lord looks at the heart.

1 Samuel 16:7

Therefore, if anyone is in Christ, he is a new creation; old things have passed away; behold, all things have become new.

2 Corinthians 5:17

And that you put on the new man which was created according to God, in true righteousness and holiness.

Ephesians 4:24

Your identity is not comprised of your actions. It isn't found in your job or economic status. It isn't because of who your family is, or what kind of personality you have. Your true identity can only be found in knowing who you are in Christ and understanding who He is in you.

You did not choose Me, but I chose you and appointed you that you should go and bear fruit, and that your fruit should remain, that whatever you ask the Father in My name He may give you.

John 15:16

You were hand-picked by God to live with a purpose He specifically designed you to fulfill. God has ordained you to bear fruit—you are destined for success (1 Peter 2:4-5, 1 Peter 2:9-10). The Spirit of God Himself lives inside of you (Romans 8:11). Christ in you is who you really are!

> *To them God willed to make known what are the riches of the glory of this mystery among the Gentiles: which is Christ in you, the hope of glory.*
>
> Colossians 1:27

Questioning Your Identity

The enemy knows that the best way to defeat you is to get you to question your true identity. The Bible tells us that he is the father of lies (John 8:44), and he will use every trick of deception he knows to make you question your identity. He doesn't have any new tricks: he uses the same strategies that he has used from the beginning of creation.

In the Garden of Eden, satan accomplished his deception by deceiving Eve into questioning the Word of God. He asked her, "Did God really say…?" (Genesis 3:1). He then got her to question her identity. He said, "For God knows that in the day you eat of it …you will be like God…" (Genesis 3:4). The truth was, Adam and Eve were both *already like God!* This trick was a total lie to get them to doubt who they truly were.

To this day, this is the devil's main strategy. He knows the power and authority you have been given, and he wants you to doubt it so that you are unable to walk in it.

When Jesus was tempted by satan in the wilderness, he also targeted Jesus' identity. He told Jesus, "If you are the Son of God…" (Luke 4:1-13). He made it seem like he was the one with all the power and authority in this world, but Jesus knew the truth. He also knew the way to resist these attacks of the devil. He responded, "It is written!" Jesus fought back with the truth found in the Word of God, and this is how we combat the lies of the enemy he throws at us as well.

> *The thief does not come except to steal, and to kill, and to destroy. I have come that they may have life, and that they may have it more abundantly.*
>
> John 10:10

Jesus made it crystal clear to us who the thief is! The devil comes to steal from you, and to try to kill and destroy you. But Jesus—who is infinitely more powerful than satan, and who proved it when He rose from the dead—came to give you abundant life!

A thief will not try to rob an empty house. Thieves don't prowl around homeless camps to steal from people who have nothing, right? The only victims of robbery are those who *already have something to steal!* You already have everything you need to walk in victory in this life! Otherwise, the devil wouldn't bother trying to take it from you.

ALL IS NOT LOST

*You already have
everything you need
to walk in victory in this life!*

Therefore, don't allow the enemy to convince you that you are a sinner, a failure, a victim, poor, weak, sick, or broken. You are the righteousness of God in Christ Jesus! You are the head and not the tail; above and not beneath; blessed and not cursed!

Leave the past behind and move into the good future God has for you.

Who Are You?

One day my husband and I were having a disagreement. I don't even remember what it was about, but I went to our bedroom in a huff and began to complain to God about Ashley. "This man that *You* gave me is…" I was so frustrated!

When I was finished ranting, I heard the Lord say, "I don't want to talk about him. Let's talk about you." The Holy Spirit began to tell me who I was in Christ and gave me scriptures that aligned with each statement. That turned into the Confession Card that our ministry provides free of charge to anyone who wants one.

The Word of God is filled with the truth of our identity as children of God.

> *Blessed be the God and Father of our Lord Jesus Christ, who has blessed us with every spiritual blessing in the heavenly places in Christ, just as He chose us in Him before the foundation of the world, that we should be holy and without blame before Him in love, having predestined us to adoption as sons by Jesus Christ to Himself, according to the good pleasure of His will, to the praise of the glory of His grace, by which He made us accepted in the Beloved.*

Ephesians 1:3-6

These four verses alone are packed full of truth regarding your true identity: already blessed with every blessing; specifically chosen by God before He even created the world; adopted as God's children and accepted in the Beloved. This passage says that all of these things are His will and give Him pleasure! Zephaniah 3:17 even tells us that God dances over us!

Sometimes we feel like we don't know what to do, or that we don't understand what we need to know. However, the Bible tells us that we already have an anointing from God and that through Him we know all things (1 John 2:20). First Corinthians 2:16 tells us that we already *have* the mind of Christ! Jesus Himself told us in advance that the Holy Spirit would teach us all things and show us things to come (John 14:26; John 16:13).

There may be times you feel that you are undeserving of the love of God. Perhaps you have identified as a "sinner" or have failed Him. However, the Word of God declares that you are the righteousness of God in Christ and that your very body is the temple of the Holy Spirit (2 Corinthians 5:21; 1 Corinthians 6:19). It says that you are anointed by God, created by Him for good works, that you have been sanctified and made holy (1 John 2:27; Ephesians 2:10; 1 Corinthians 6:11). Romans 8:28-30 even says that God predestined you to succeed!

The Bible tells us that no matter what circumstances in which you may find yourself, you are blessed! You are the head and not the tail, above and not beneath (Deuteronomy 28:13). No weapon formed against you can prosper, and you have been given victory wherever you go (Isaiah 54:17; 2 Corinthians 2:14). Since God is for you, nothing can come against you and succeed (Romans 8:31).

…As He is, so are we in this world.

1 John 4:17

If you understand who the Word of God says you really are, when the enemy lies to you, it will have no effect. You will know that no matter how you feel, or what it looks like, this is the truth. You were created to live a successful, abundant life! Then you can successfully use the Word of God to fight back against those lies, speak the truth over your situation, and receive the victory.

Subdue and Take Dominion

I thought about this idea of our identity, and how it influences our ability to reign and rule, many years later while watching bears prowl through our back yard, nosing their way into our trailer. At first sight, they took me by surprise, and I contemplated my options. Deciding that calling animal control to remove them would take too long—and by that time our trailer could be in shreds—it suddenly dawned on me that I have been given authority over the earth, with the power to subdue everything in it.

> *God said, Let Us [Father, Son, and Holy Spirit] make mankind in Our image, after Our likeness, and let them have complete authority over the fish of the sea, the birds of the air, the [tame] beasts, and over all of the earth, and over everything that creeps upon the earth. So God created man in His own image, in the image and likeness of God He created him; male and*

female He created them. And God blessed them and said to them, Be fruitful, multiply, and fill the earth, and subdue it [using all its vast resources in the service of God and man]; and have dominion over the fish of the sea, the birds of the air, and over every living creature that moves upon the earth.

Genesis 1:26-28 AMPC

Subduing seemed the logical choice, so I did what any mama bear would do while trying to protect her own little cubs: I shouted at the top of my lungs and told that mama bear to turn around and leave, along with her baby. I'd like to say that being the woman of faith and power than I am in Jesus, that I never doubted.

However, I was still amazed when that mama bear looked up in my direction, shrugged her shoulders and climbed out of the trailer, followed by her cub. Even though the bear weighed hundreds of pounds, and one swipe of those big paws could eliminate little me in a heartbeat, she just didn't want to mess with this mama bear!

Looking for a snack, those huge powerful creatures are too lazy to go very far. Bears roam around in the autumn months looking for as many things to eat as they can find without putting in too much effort. Yet with an assertive tone of voice, that bear ambled off—irritated by the disturbance and the extra effort she had to exert in order to get the snack she was hoping for.

Despite the credit that many believers give him, satan does not have perseverance as a fruit of his spirit. He has no new tricks. He is just a master recycler—all he can do is recycle old lies because he has nothing new. He can't create anything. With this lack of creativity and perseverance, he has learned to move on when faced with resistance.

> *Be sober, be vigilant; because your adversary the devil walks about like a roaring lion, seeking whom he may devour. Resist him, steadfast in the faith, knowing that the same sufferings are experienced by your brotherhood in the world.*
>
> 1 Peter 5:8-9

The Word of God works. We have been given authority over the things of this earth.

We have been given authority
over the things of this earth.

Using Our Authority

Our authority was given to us by God to be used against every wile of the enemy! As an underdog, the authority that God has given you is an irreplaceable tool to be used on your path to victory.

> *Therefore submit to God. Resist the devil and he will flee from you.*

> James 4:7

This scripture is so powerful. It shows us that we have power and authority over the enemy to the point where he will literally take off running. It also describes how this authority thing works, and both elements are key to seeing authority work effectively.

Submit to God

Submission is not a popular word in today's culture, and for those of whom submission has been demanded it can bring back terrifying memories. *Submit* here is the Greek word *hypotasso*. It means "to become subordinate to, to obey, to bring yourself under the authority, admonition, or advice of another." The very essence of the word is a choice. If someone *forces* you submit, then it's not really submission, it is control.

So let's make sure we don't confuse control and submission. Control forces a person against their will; it restrains and brings uniformity outside of choice. Submission places another person in a position of authority and says, "I'm with them. Whatever they decide, I will follow." It is used in scripture a couple of different ways. One is as a military term, meaning to arrange in a military troop under a commanding officer. Another way it is used is as a voluntary attitude of giving in, cooperating, assuming responsibility and carrying a burden.

Submission is powerful when we submit to the right things. Submitting to God, who we know loves us unconditionally and has the best planned for us, becomes easy once we know Him. Many people submit to God out of fear and control and never really see their God-given authority working because their motivation is not faith but fear.

> Submission is powerful when we submit to the right things.

When we submit to God by saying, "I'm with You. Whatever You say, Lord, that will I believe and that will I follow," then you have the devil scared.

When people saw Jesus, they recognized Him as a man of authority, and His teachings as those with authority. When Jesus met the centurion in Matthew 8:7-10, the centurion saw that Jesus was a man under authority. He understood that authority comes from true submission.

Yet Jesus, although God, was also one hundred percent man. He had authority on earth the same way we do—by submitting to His Father. He said, "I only do what I see my Father doing, be it on earth as it in in heaven. Not My will be done, but Yours." Jesus had to submit His flesh to the Word of God in order for His authority to be recognized.

We have authority over everything in this world that is contrary to the Word of God. Any work of the devil recognizes you as a child of God, and the minute you submit to who God says you are, the devil is in trouble.

God has given us the choice to submit to Him. If He demanded it, we would not have free will or the ability to mess up. We would be robots controlled by an autocratic, narcissistic dictator. But God so loved us that He gave us His Son so that whoever chooses to believe in Him should not perish but have everlasting life (John 3:16). What kind of life? Abundant life, here on the earth first, and later in Heaven.

It's easy to choose to submit to God when we see how much He loves us. In fact, there is great security knowing that we are part of the army of God as believers, sharing the burden, a community of heaven, with a commanding officer who guides our very path and stands with us in every battle. Now, that portrays quite a different picture than what some of us may have experienced.

The other aspect of real submission is equally unpopular, but while we're here, we might as well go there!

Obedience

Obedience! Yes, that thing we all want our kids to understand but don't really always want to model ourselves. Obedience is the fruit of submission; it is an important aspect of a submitted heart. When someone's heart is submitted to God, you can see it in their actions. They follow God's Word and choose to believe it above the circumstances. A submitted heart will walk out a life of faith, and you'll see the fruit of the spirit in their life. They are people centered in peace; they are humble.

When someone's heart is submitted to God, you can see it in their actions.

Many people struggle to obey, but why? Simply, they haven't *chosen* to submit their hearts to God in some areas. They have some pride and maybe some hyper independence because they have been neglected. There may be a need to be in control because they have been out of control or controlled by another at some point in their lives.

Everyone has stuff in the corners of their heart—you know, the dark ugly places that come up to say hello every now and then. We would call it a bad attitude, defensive, overreacting, emotional, having a fear of missing out, arrogant, touchy, jealous, selfish, or rebellious.

These are all symptoms of an unsubmitted heart. And if you have ever been "lost" at some point, you have probably used some of these as coping mechanisms to hide your pain rather than submitting it to God. The danger is, a heart that is unsubmitted to God will end up submitting to something else, because we were designed with the capacity to submit.

Rebellion Is Witchcraft

My heart became emotionally shut down after trauma; hyper independence, self-sufficiency, and rebellion began in the literal form of witchcraft. Entertaining powers not of God swung wide the door to the enemy working in my body, almost to the point of death several times.

Some people think this can't happen to a true man or woman of God. Well, it happened to King Saul! He was God's first choice before David, but unlike David, Saul's heart was not submitted to God. He lied to cover his mistakes rather than repent like David did. Saul was more submitted to the opinions of others than what God said about him. He bowed to pressure, lost his kingdom, and fell into witchcraft (1 Samuel 15:22-23). And it all started with an unsubmitted heart. Scripture says that rebellion is as the sin of witchcraft.

The condition of my heart—through no fault of my own—became fertile ground for the work of the enemy. The victim mindset is like an incubator for every evil work. It is extremely damaging to the individual and those around them. Only the strong will break free from it, even though freedom is available, because the temporary comfort that it brings is so inviting. Change happens in hearts when the pain of staying in the pit becomes greater than the effort required to climb out of it.

> *Change happens in hearts when the pain of staying in the pit becomes greater than the effort required to climb out of it.*

So, what if we see that we have some funk going on in our heart and we want to be free from it and start to see the power and authority of God flow through us? James 4:1-10 (MEV) has a lot to say about this:

> *Where do wars and fights among you come from? Do they not come from your lusts that war in your*

body? You lust and do not have, so you kill. You desire to have and cannot obtain. You fight and war. Yet you do not have, because you do not ask. You ask, and do not receive, because you ask amiss, that you may spend it on your passions. You adulterers and adulteresses, do you not know that the friendship with the world is enmity with God? Whoever therefore will be a friend of the world is the enemy of God. Do you think that the Scripture says in vain, "He yearns jealously for the spirit that lives in us"? But He gives more grace. For this reason it says: "God resists the proud, but gives grace to the humble." Therefore submit yourselves to God. Resist the devil, and he will flee from you. Draw near to God, and He will draw near to you. Cleanse your hands, you sinners, and purify your hearts, you double-minded. Grieve and mourn and weep. Let your laughter be turned to mourning, and your joy to dejection. Humble yourselves in the sight of the Lord, and He will lift you up.

We don't have authority because we ask amiss, asking and not seeing. Wow. This lays it out: we don't see the results of our authority when we speak at times because our heart is not submitted. Rather, it contains pride. Pride is the fruit of rebellion, like obedience is the fruit of submission.

This passage says that God resists the proud. Our pride is a form of resistance, but it is us resisting God! We don't want to find ourselves resisting God. It is much better to resist the devil and submit to God, as we read back in James 4:7.

But check out verse six: He gives grace to the humble! When we humble ourselves before God, we own our bad attitudes rather than making excuses for them. I don't know about you, but anytime I have more than one reason for something, I know I'm making excuses.

No matter what circumstances caused the ugly to be in my heart, I don't want it opening my life to the power of the enemy. Instead, I confess it and crush it! Repenting of our sin—changing our mind and turning the other way—it isn't the first time God finds out about it.

He waits for us to invite Him into the situation, like a parent restraining themselves from trying to hit the brakes when their child is learning to drive. (Teaching a teen to drive does wonders for your prayer life!) Humility is submitting to and agreeing with what God says. I have learned that when I find I have been resisting God to repent and let Him in. That is the first step in having a heart submitted to God.

Resist the Enemy

Authority is not passive, lazy, nor silent. When we know in whom we have believed, and the power that's backing us up as children of God, resisting the enemy becomes natural. In other words, it is part of our nature. In a monarchy, if a peasant tried to tell a prince how to rule, the royal would respond, "Wait just a minute, here. Who do you think you are?" Our authority over the enemy, and our resistance to him, is just as natural of a response.

> *Be sober, be vigilant; because your adversary the devil walks about like a roaring lion, seeking whom he may devour. Resist him, steadfast in the faith...*
>
> 1 Peter 5:8-9

Resist means to actively stand against. Yes, the enemy is roaming around looking for his next meal, but he is going to wish he'd never bumped into *you*. Why? Because you are like a dog with a bone—you just won't let go. That's the steadfast part that Peter talks about. Outlast the enemy by holding onto the promises of God like your life depends on it—because it does! There is an element of persistence involved. We *will* win if we don't quit.

We will win if we don't quit.

Authority and Identity

Remember the examples of Prince George, and a peasant trying to tell a royal how to rule? A royal knows exactly who they are. They know their position is secured by birthright. In the same way, we were chosen by God and adopted as His children. We are royal, and knowing the truth of our identity helps us to step into our authority more effectively.

Security in our identity comes through knowing who God is and how He sees us: as chosen, beloved, accepted, righteous, holy, and fully equipped. By acknowledging who He is in us—as victorious, as an overcomer, as more than a conqueror—we begin to see the role that identity plays in the outcomes of life's challenges.

We really must major on confessing who we are in Christ simply because we need to hear the truth of who we are over and over again. The world is confused about identity. Therefore, it tries to push its identity crisis on to us. It is vital that as believers we find our identity in the Word of God, alone.

The Word of God has saved my life—both in this life and the next—and it is not confused. Here is an identity truth bomb found directly in the scriptures: there are two genders and one race. Confusion to these realities creeps in when we begin to misalign our identity to something outside of who God says we are.

The moment we look for temporary things in the world to define us, the enemy cheers. He hates us 'cause he ain't us! We are the only creatures God created in His image, with His name and His authority. As an angel, having not been given those rights, it bent Lucifer so badly out of shape that he rebelled and became satan. So, having a clear understanding of how God sees you, and identifying with that picture, is instrumental in walking in the authority that we have been given.

We are the only creatures God created in His image, with His name and His authority.

Lessons from Moses

Moses is a test case of identity crisis. A Hebrew baby, the son of slaves, raised as royalty in an Egyptian palace. As much as his environment, and those around him, tried to squeeze him into their version of who they thought he should be, he couldn't escape who he really was.

He was a Hebrew, supernaturally preserved and nurtured by his own kin through a divine encounter. A child once sentenced to death by the very people who later accepted him into their home and raised him in opulence. Yet, all the while baby Moses was growing, his mother was whispering in his ear the stories of their God.

As a man, Moses saw the disparity between the world he had come from and the world in which he was raised. The tension eventually reached a breaking point and Moses killed an Egyptian in defense of one of his own.

> *Then he said, "Who made you a prince and a judge over us? Do you intend to kill me as you killed the Egyptian?"*

Exodus 2:14

It was a fair question, and the witness made it clear that they knew Moses was leading a double life. He chose his side with his actions and fled. Now, not fitting with either culture, he wandered to a place far away where no one would know him. Many of us can relate to this. It's often easier to start over than face the past or work on relationships that have become difficult.

For example, church hoppers have this perfected. They are all in until they are challenged in some way—not wanting to submit to authority within a church, or not wanting to submit financially in the area of giving, so they make a quick exit. Although, the story usually sounds something like, "Well, they just didn't recognize my gifting," or, "The pastor is too controlling," or, "We just felt called to leave right after we announced that we would be there forever." All of which could be true but are also characteristic of classic submission issues. This is a pattern that we will want to address if we recognize this developing, as it will hinder our personal and spiritual growth.

However, even though he ran, Moses couldn't hide. He knew deep down who he belonged to, whose family he was a part of. God met Moses on the back side of the desert and called him. Moses didn't take it well. His insecurities showed as he had a back and forth with God Almighty, coming up with every excuse why he wasn't the man for the job. Again, another place where we can probably all relate. Who hasn't played "Deal or No Deal" at some point in their prayer time? Spiritual bargaining at its best!

So, God called Moses by name and picked him to go back to those he had run from and deliver the Hebrews from the oppression of the Egyptians. You can see why Moses had reservations—this was an awkward family reunion on steroids.

Moses asked God a question:

> *Who am I that I should go to Pharaoh, and that I should bring the children of Israel out of Egypt?*
>
> Exodus 3:11

God didn't answer the question because the fact that *He* was with Moses made it irrelevant. There is no heritage, no title, no principality or power greater than God Himself. If God saying, "I'm with him" isn't enough, then what is?!

But Moses didn't get it. He literally spent the whole chapter trying to get out of it! The Lord was so patient with Moses. Personally, I would have drop-kicked him, but thankfully God didn't involve me! So, rather than nuking Moses, God reassured him, set him in a team, equipped him, trained him and told him the plan.

Then after Moses agreed to go, God told him, "All those who sought to kill you are dead" (Exodus 4:19). It's no coincidence that He didn't divulge this nugget of information earlier. It wasn't like God just found out. Moses needed to learn that he could trust God with him, even in the face of adversity. God is not into bargaining or twisting our arms to believe Him. He speaks and moves by the language of faith.

Over the next few chapters in the book of Exodus, you can see Moses growing in confidence, beginning to walk as a child of God rather than as a misfit, stateless nomad. The ten plagues pass, and Moses leads the people out of Egypt all the way to the edge of the Red Sea. Pinned against the sea, and under serious pressure from the Egyptians in hot pursuit, Moses steps up. He doesn't sound like the same guy who met with God at the burning bush. There is nothing timid about a man who knows God is on his side. Boldness came upon him, and he gave a speech worthy of a presidential candidate on the final night of debates. If he was running today, I'd vote for him!

And Moses said to the people, "Do not be afraid.
Stand still, and see the salvation of the Lord, which
He will accomplish for you today. For the Egyptians

*whom you see today, you shall see again no more for-
ever. The Lord will fight for you, and you shall hold
your peace."*

Exodus 14:13-14

This was a rally cry! You can imagine all the people going
from desperation and hopelessness, watching the Egyptian
chariots approaching, to sudden jubilation and expectation of
deliverance. They expected another miracle like the plagues
they had just witnessed. Except this time, it was different.

*And the Lord said to Moses, "Why do you cry to Me?
Tell the children of Israel to go forward. But lift up
your rod, and stretch out your hand over the sea and
divide it. And the children of Israel shall go on dry
ground through the midst of the sea."*

Exodus 14:15-16

This time, Moses had to use the authority he had been given.
It was God's stamp of approval on Moses in front of the children of Israel. Moses was ready. He had been equipped, tested,
and approved. All that was left was for Moses to stretch out his
hand and dispense the power and authority which God had
given him.

Moses got to witness some of the greatest miracles in history. He was entrusted with the written Word of God, he set
up the government of nations, and led millions to freedom.

This from a guy who was once afraid to go and face the music, whose inner demons and insecurities caused him to question God's decisions.

The truth is, we can't run far enough, hide deep enough, or mess up badly enough to exclude ourselves from His redemptive power. There is no sorry loser who God hasn't called to be a conqueror. God has given us so much more than Moses had. We have a Bible full of promises, an unbreakable covenant relationship with God Himself, signed in blood by Jesus so we couldn't mess it up. We have the Holy Spirit who gets down in the pit with us and partners with us to remove every hinderance and lead us to safety.

> There is no sorry loser who God hasn't called to be a conqueror.

We have a full spiritual armor to deflect attacks of the enemy, a spiritual language that gives us a direct line to the power of God, and delegated authority in the name of Jesus to heal the sick, cast out devils and raise the dead (Luke 9:1; Matthew 10:1, 8). The only thing stopping us from succeeding in every area of life is the fuzz between our ears!

Chapter Eight

Changing Perspective

As an underdog making a comeback—realizing that all is not lost, moving forward on your path from trauma to victory—once you have an understanding of your true identity, and begin to see yourself the way God sees you, it is necessary to begin to see your circumstances from God's perspective as well.

For centuries, the human race has had to overcome adversity to survive. What sets apart the victors from the victims is their perspective. Victors prepare for victory by looking at negative circumstances and seeing the victory ahead.

In other words, how we view challenges determines our ability to overcome them. Proverbs 23:7 says, *"As he thinks in his heart, so is he."* The way we imagine a situation to play out is often a self-fulfilling prophesy.

When our son goes out on the soccer field and his team scores the first goal of the match, their chances of holding the score line and winning the game increases. The confidence level in the team gets a boost, and suddenly, they believe that they can win. When they believe that they can win they begin to play like they can win.

I have watched those boys go out against much bigger and stronger teams and beat them easily because they could see the victory. Physical preparation and training are obviously important, but mental preparation is the secret weapon that separates the victims from the victors.

The Lord sees our circumstances differently than the world does because He sees us differently than we see ourselves. He says that we are world overcomers.

> *For whatever is born of God overcomes the world. And this is the victory that has overcome the world— our faith.*
>
> 1 John 5:4

He says that there is no challenge that can destroy us.

> *No weapon formed against you shall prosper, And every tongue which rises against you in judgment You shall condemn.*
>
> Isaiah 54:17

God says that nothing we have done, are about to do, or will do in the future has the power to separate us from His love.

> *Who shall separate us from the love of Christ? Shall tribulation, or distress, or persecution, or famine, or nakedness, or peril, or sword? As it is written:*

"For Your sake we are killed all day long; We are accounted as sheep for the slaughter." Yet in all these things we are more than conquerors through Him who loved us. For I am persuaded that neither death nor life, nor angels nor principalities nor powers, nor things present nor things to come, nor height nor depth, nor any other created thing, shall be able to separate us from the love of God which is in Christ Jesus our Lord.

Romans 8:35-37

The Lord tells us that we have faith enough to move mountains.

So Jesus answered and said to them, "Have faith in God. For assuredly, I say to you, whoever says to this mountain, 'Be removed and be cast into the sea,' and does not doubt in his heart, but believes that those things he says will be done, he will have whatever he says."

Mark 11:22-23

These are the truths that help us to change our perspective and begin to see ourselves—and our circumstances—the way that God sees them. He didn't create us for defeat. We were designed for victory!

Gaining Proper Perspective

Being five-foot-nothing and built like a twig, I was as surprised as anyone when my high school athletic coach decided that I should run hurdles and enter the high jump.

The hurdles themselves came up to my chest, each topped with a thick wooden plank designed to inflict maximum bruising on any short or lazy-legged individual who attempted to leap over them. I hated them all indiscriminately. My knees were blue and swollen and the more I focused on not crashing into them the more the crashing happened.

Crouching side by side with my teammates, my feet barely touched the metal foot plates on the starting line, even at full stretch. While their long spider legs were squished up under them, ready to burst forth and leap the entire hurdle set in a single bound, I guessed I was absent when the long-legged genes were being dished out. I saw those hurdles as insurmountable obstacles that my size made impossible to overcome.

Apparently, Coach saw in me a quality that was more important for success than the limitations of my physical stature. Rather than adjust my physical technique, I needed a perspective adjustment. Coach's advice was to focus on the finish line, rather than on the next hurdle in front of me. It was not the obstacle that determined the outcome of the event, but rather how I viewed the obstacle.

The Lord sees our circumstances differently than the world does, because He sees us differently than we do. He says that we are world overcomers, that no weapon formed against us will prosper, that we have faith enough to move mountains, and that life and death are in the power of our tongues. How we respond to situations—what comes out when we are squeezed—depends on how we have chosen to see them.

How we respond to situations depends on how we have chosen to see them.

The Importance of Perspective

Our perspective has a huge effect on our physical bodies, our mental well-being, our performance, our relationships—everything. Proverbs 23:7 says that as a man *"thinks in his heart, so is he."* We become the people we imagine ourselves to be, whether victims or victors. If we imagine ourselves as winners, champions, overcomers, prosperous, and healed, that is who we will be! However, if we imagine ourselves as sick, poor, and defeated, then that is what we will see in our lives.

Throughout our lives, we will experience change. However, there is one thing that is unchanging and absolute: Jesus! We are who God says we are, we have what He says we have, and we can do what He says we can do—if we can only wrap our minds around His Word enough that we allow it to transform us (Romans 12:1-2).

Circumstances change, storms pass over, and scars heal, but unless we take time to deal with the aftereffects of trials in our souls, we can remain stuck in them long after they have finished.

For example, elephants taken as a calves and chained to tree, with nothing more than a bicycle wheel on a rope to scare them, learn not to pull on the rope to get away. Fear of that bicycle wheel will keep the elephant bound to the tree long after it has become full grown, more than able to break free.

In Numbers 13, twelve Israelites were sent to spy out the land that the Lord was giving them. The spies went on a recon mission to devise a plan to take the promised land: not *if* they could take it, but *how*. Moses didn't ask them to find out all of the obstacles. They were meant to simply gather information so that a plan of attack could be made. The report that came back, though, was less than optimistic:

> *Then Caleb quieted the people before Moses, and said, "Let us go up at once and take possession, for we are well able to overcome it." But the men who had gone up with him said, "We are not able to go up against the people, for they are stronger than we." And they gave the children of Israel a bad report of the land*

which they had spied out, saying, "The land through
which we have gone as spies is a land that devours
its inhabitants, and all the people whom we saw in it
are men of great stature. There we saw the giants (the
descendants of Anak came from the giants); and we
were like grasshoppers in our own sight, and so we
were in their sight."

Numbers 13:30-33

Ten of the men saw the giants in the land and saw them
as an obstacle that would be impossible to overcome. In fact,
they saw themselves as grasshoppers in the face of these giants!
Their grasshopper vision infected those around them and kept
the entire nation from inheriting God's promises. Instead of
going in and taking the land God had given them, they instead
wandered the desert for forty years, until the generation of
unbelievers had died!

Only Joshua and Caleb could see past the problems. These
two men had a different spirit within them—they were victorious in their minds first. They were "how-to" people, not "if"
people. Joshua and Caleb knew that no matter how weak the
Israelites seemed to be in the natural—compared to the giants—
God was the one who had promised them this land and that He
would enable their victory. They decided that they were well able
to go in and possess the land the Lord had promised them!

Forty years later, the truth of the situation came to light.
Moses had died, and it was time for Joshua to lead the children

of Israel into the promised land. He sent two spies to survey the land, especially the city of Jericho. While in Jericho, the spies came to the home of a woman, Rahab. She revealed to them the truth of how the people of the land had actually viewed the Israelites.

> ... *I know that the Lord has given you the land, that the terror of you has fallen on us, and that all the inhabitants of the land are fainthearted because of you. For we have heard how the Lord dried up the water of the Red Sea for you when you came out of Egypt, and what you did to the two kings of the Amorites who were on the other side of the Jordan, Sihon and Og, whom you utterly destroyed. **And as soon as we heard these things, our hearts melted; neither did there remain any more courage in anyone because of you, for the Lord your God, He is God in heaven above and on earth beneath.***

Joshua 2:9-11 (emphasis added)

You see, the ten original spies had seen the strength of the people of the land and assumed that the Canaanites shared their own grasshopper vision. In fact, the opposite was true! The people of Canaan were *terrified* of the Israelites because they had heard the stories of all that God had done for them. If the Israelites had been obedient the first time—while those stories were fresh in the minds of the Canaanites—perhaps their enemies would have just fled in terror *without any bloodshed at all.*

Overcoming grasshopper vision begins with a decision to look beyond the circumstances of today to the future and the promises that the Lord has already set in motion for us. There may be giants in the land, but we are well able to overcome them and possess all of God's promises!

There may be giants in the land, but we are well able to overcome them and possess all of God's promises!

Remember Who Is in Your Boat

Many times, when we are facing a challenging life circumstance, we look at what is going on around us and take our eyes off Jesus. Our natural minds have been conditioned to view our situations from a merely natural perspective. However, when in the middle of a storm, it is important to remember who is in your boat with you!

When Jesus was still with the disciples, He gave them very clear instructions regarding their purpose and the authority they were to use in His name. He *"called His twelve disciples* together and gave them power and authority over all demons, and to cure diseases. He sent them to preach the kingdom of God and to heal the sick" (Luke 9:1-2).

> And these signs will follow those who believe: In My name they will cast out demons; they will speak with new tongues; they will take up serpents; and if they drink anything deadly, it will by no means hurt them; they will lay hands on the sick, and they will recover.
>
> Mark 16:17-18

However, the disciples still struggled to grasp the extent of the power Jesus had given them. The truth of this was displayed one night when they faced a brutal storm.

> On the same day, when evening had come, He said to them, "Let us cross over to the other side." And a great windstorm arose, and the waves beat into the boat, so that it was already filling. But He was in the stern, asleep on a pillow. And they awoke Him and said to Him, "Teacher, do You not care that we are perishing?" Then He arose and rebuked the wind, and said to the sea, "Peace, be still!" And the wind ceased and there was a great calm. But He said to them, "Why are you so fearful? How is it that you have no faith?" And they feared exceedingly, and said to one another, "Who can this be, that even the wind and the sea obey Him!"
>
> Mark 4:35-41

The disciples didn't realize that *God* was in the boat with them! Jesus had informed the disciples they were using the boat to cross to the other side of the lake. Jesus expected the storm, but it was irrelevant. The result of their journey—arriving on the other side safely—was a foregone conclusion. Although Jesus knew the storm was coming, He still told the disciples to go. They were going to make it! Jesus would not have told them to do something that they could not achieve.

However, during the storm, the disciples (not yet grounded in faith) went from, "Ooh, this could be scary," to "God, help! We're going to die!" They took their eyes off Jesus and focused on their surroundings. In fact, they even accused Jesus of not caring about them!

Then, the moment Jesus calmed the storm, the disciples were astounded at His authority. They did not fully appreciate who was with them in the boat or the authority He had given them. Truthfully, the disciples didn't need Jesus' help that night! They had everything within themselves to get across that lake; they just didn't realize it.

Another storm gave the disciples an opportunity to step out in faith. Again, they were out on the sea in a boat, while a storm raged.

Now in the fourth watch of the night Jesus went to them, walking on the sea. And when the disciples saw Him walking on the sea, they were troubled, saying, "It is a ghost!" And they cried out for fear. But immediately Jesus spoke to them, saying, "Be of good cheer!

ALL IS NOT LOST

It is I; do not be afraid." And Peter answered Him and said, "Lord, if it is You, command me to come to You on the water."

So He said, "Come." And when Peter had come down out of the boat, he walked on the water to go to Jesus. But when he saw that the wind was boisterous, he was afraid; and beginning to sink he cried out, saying, "Lord, save me!" And immediately Jesus stretched out His hand and caught him, and said to him, "O you of little faith, why did you doubt?" And when they got into the boat, the wind ceased.

Matthew 14:25-32

Peter only began to sink when he allowed the storm to distract Him. Jesus was right there, within reach. Yet Peter allowed the fact that the waves were crashing around him to take his eyes off Jesus and make him afraid.

He was already walking on the water! That miracle alone should have given Peter a *huge* level of confidence and courage. But that's what circumstances do. They distract us to get our eyes off Jesus, even though He is right there with us!

Storms will come. In fact, Jesus promised they will (John 16:33). However, even in the middle of a storm, remember who is in your boat! Jesus will never leave or forsake you. He is always with you, and His Spirit lives inside of you. He has given you all the power to overcome! Don't get distracted. Keep your eyes on Jesus, and He will keep you in peace.

You will keep him in perfect peace, Whose mind is stayed on You, Because he trusts in You.

Isaiah 26:3

Victory Starts in Your Mind

David had a decision to make when he heard the news about the giant the Israelite army was facing. Goliath had stated his claim and spewed his words of intimidation against the armies of Israel. To Goliath's credit, those threats he made were not empty words—this was a man of war who had taken down many before. He was the champion of the enemy armies.

The Philistines stood on a mountain on one side, and Israel stood on a mountain on the other side, with a valley between them. And a champion went out from the camp of the Philistines, named Goliath, from Gath, whose height was six cubits and a span. He had a bronze helmet on his head, and he was armed with a coat of mail, and the weight of the coat was five thousand shekels of bronze. And he had bronze armor on his legs and a bronze javelin between his shoulders. Now the staff of his spear was like a weaver's beam, and his iron spearhead weighed six hundred shekels; and a shield-bearer went before him. Then he stood and cried out to the armies of Israel, and said to them, "Why have you come out to line up for battle? Am I not a Philistine, and you the servants of Saul? Choose a man for yourselves, and let him come down to me. If he is able to fight with me and kill me, then we will be your servants. But if I prevail against him and kill him, then you shall be our servants and serve us." And the Philistine said, "I defy the armies of Israel this day; give me a man, that we may fight together."

1 Samuel 17:3-10

To put this battle in perspective, the invading Philistine army had made camp, and every day for forty days they sent their champion out to face off with the men of Israel. Every day the soldiers had heard the threats from the enemy camp, and every day they looked at Goliath's great stature and were aware of their own frailty.

Then as he talked with them, there was the champion, the Philistine of Gath, Goliath by name, coming up from the armies of the Philistines; and he spoke according to the same words. So David heard them. And all the men of Israel, when they saw the man, fled from him and were dreadfully afraid.

1 Samuel 17:23-24

David hadn't been invited to the party. He was a youth, the youngest of all his brothers and had been left home to feed the sheep. The only reason he was at the battle line that day was to bring supplies up to the troops. David heard Goliath's threats and saw his great stature, just the same as the actual soldiers did that day, but he had a different reaction to it.

David was outraged. "Is there not a cause?!" he demanded of those who were running in fear. David was not looking at his own ability to overcome that experienced man of war. He did not consider his own weakness, or the failure of those who had gone before him. The underdog in David rose up in the face of adversity because David knew something the others didn't. David had a covenant relationship with the God of Israel and this giant was in direct violation of His children.

> *Then David spoke to the men who stood by him, saying, "What shall be done for the man who kills this Philistine and takes away the reproach from Israel? For who is this uncircumcised Philistine, that he should defy the armies of the living God?"*
>
> 1 Samuel 17:26

Victory in David's mind was not determined by the size of an army but by the size of his God. David had a history with God, a God who was faithful and ever present to deliver him.

> *Then David said to Saul, "Let no man's heart fail because of him; your servant will go and fight with this Philistine." And Saul said to David, "You are not able to go against this Philistine to fight with him; for*

*you are a youth, and he a man of war from his youth."
But David said to Saul, "Your servant used to keep
his father's sheep, and when a lion or a bear came
and took a lamb out of the flock, I went out after it
and struck it, and delivered the lamb from its mouth;
and when it arose against me, I caught it by its beard,
and struck and killed it. Your servant has killed both
lion and bear; and this uncircumcised Philistine will
be like one of them, seeing he has defied the armies
of the living God." Moreover David said, "The Lord,
who delivered me from the paw of the lion and from
the paw of the bear, He will deliver me from the hand
of this Philistine."*

1 Samuel 17:32-37

Victory in David's mind was not determined by the size of an army but by the size of his God.

Goliath overstepped his authority by messing with the children of God, but he didn't see defeat until one of them was able to see their victory. You see how outmatched the devil is when he comes out against us? All it took to defeat the biggest, strongest champion in history was one little shepherd boy who knew what it meant to have God on his side.

> All it took to defeat the biggest, strongest champion in history was one little shepherd boy who knew what it meant to have God on his side.

The attitude of the underdog doesn't quit. When circumstances were looking the worst, and even his family didn't believe in him, David put his trust in God. He saw the situation according to God's perspective, rather than the fear of the rest of the Israelite army. David's authority was evident in the words that he spoke and the actions that followed.

Then David said to the Philistine, "You come to me with a sword, with a spear, and with a javelin. But I come to you in the name of the Lord of hosts, the God of the armies of Israel, whom you have defied. This day the Lord will deliver you into my hand, and I will strike you and take your head from you. And this day I will give the carcasses of the camp of the Philistines to the birds of the air and the wild beasts of the earth, that all the earth may know that there is a God in Israel. Then all this assembly shall know that the Lord does not save with sword and spear; for the battle is the Lord's, and He will give you into our hands."

1 Samuel 17:45-47

David shouted right back at that giant and told him exactly how this battle was going to end. He declared his victory with every step he took toward the enemy. He ran at that giant with his mouth open and the end result in mind. Notice that he didn't run away from the giant, phone a friend or get the measuring tape of comparison out to see whether it looked like he could beat that giant or not.

David looked way beyond how he felt about the challenge, past the failure of previous applicants in the battle, and evicted any thoughts of doubt or inadequacy. He could never match up to the might and experience of Goliath, but he didn't have to, because the battle was not his. The battle was the Lord's.

David's victory over Goliath was not won on the battlefield, it was won in his mind before he ever showed up at the front lines.

Giant killers like David see the victory before the challenge and keep it as their focus. This enables them to move past the trial and emerge victorious on the other side. The victory was so real to David that it gave him the courage to run headfirst at that giant with the full assurance that, with God, he was well able to overcome it. The mental picture David had was so real, in fact, that David described in great detail to Goliath exactly what victory looked like and how it was going to come about!

David's victory over Goliath was not won on the battlefield, it was won in his mind before he ever showed up at the front lines.

Some battles have hung around so long that we forget how to fight them or are so conditioned to a particular response that we follow what everyone else is doing without thinking about it. But who said that we need to be afraid of sickness and disease? Who said that we don't have enough to live on? Who said that we shouldn't get our hopes up? Who said not

ALL IS NOT LOST

to expect too much? *Who said?* Sounds to me like an enemy intimidation tactic!

Our Goliaths today might have different names, but the battle plan hasn't changed. Practice your battle cry, see the victory beyond the giant, and crush defeat before it has opportunity to speak!

Chapter Nine

Controlling Our Thoughts

Hopefully, by this point, you've decided to begin to see your circumstances from God's perspective: all is not lost, those challenges are not impossible to overcome, and God has fully equipped you to walk in victory over them! Even though you have this revelation and have made this decision, there will still be plenty of opportunity for you to become distracted and take your eyes off Jesus.

Controlling our thoughts is a challenge that will present itself consistently throughout our lives. However, God has given us the grace and power—through faith in His power within us—to redirect our thoughts and keep our eyes stayed upon Him and view our world from His perspective. We just need to be aware these challenges will come and prepare ourselves for victory!

Being prepared is key to survival. If you don't believe this, just hit the remote and count the reality television shows on the topic! Before lunch, you can learn everything from how to build your own cabin and live off the land in deepest Alaska

ALL IS NOT LOST

to the art of churning your own butter and ten useful items to make out of an old flowerpot.

But wait! Put the pitchfork and shovel down. Before you rush out to the yard to pick your ideal bunker location to survive impending doom, let's think this through.

There is a factor that is often overlooked by those determined to prepare for life after a nuclear fallout, national disaster, or zombie apocalypse. God has a plan for our lives that is not shipwreck-able by any outside force, but by us alone.

God has a plan for our lives that is not shipwreck-able by any outside force, but by us alone.

Our battle is not over the circumstances of life because our faith already gave us the victory over the things of this world (1 John 5:4). The preparation I'm talking about starts between our ears.

> *For though we walk in the flesh, we do not war according to the flesh. For the weapons of our warfare are not carnal but mighty in God for pulling down*

strongholds, casting down arguments and every high thing that exalts itself against the knowledge of God, bringing every thought into captivity to the obedience of Christ.

2 Corinthians 10:3-5

Taking Control of the Crazy

When our kids were little, trying to keep them on task and contained was always a challenge! Having three children under three years old could be likened to raising goats. In many ways they are similar, and if you have ever ventured into a supermarket with a cart full of toddlers, you will know exactly what I'm talking about!

By the time you arrive at the checkout to pay for the now empty boxes—because goats numbers one and two have already eaten their contents—goat number three needs rescuing from the display rack they mounted while your attention was on the other two! Little ones can have the ability to bring a sane adult to their knees in a matter of minutes.

Our thoughts remind me of those toddler moments. If we don't contain them, they can get wild and crazy pretty quickly! They consume our time, energy and emotions as our feelings begin to follow whatever we have been thinking on.

Worry, anxiety, fear, and depression are emotions that everyone *must* experience at some point—you can't help it, right?

ALL IS NOT LOST

Wrong! That's a lie which is not based in Scripture at all but has become so common in the world today that we can be fooled into thinking it's normal.

God does not want us to be slaves to negative emotions. Take fear, for example. It seems that the world is increasingly driven to action based in fear. Yet, as believers, our lives should not be driven by fear, but by faith in our loving Father God.

> *Perfect love casts out fear, because fear involves torment.*
>
> 1 John 4:18

There is only one tormentor: the devil. Through his deceptive tormenting tactics, he tries to draw our focus away from the truth of God's promises. He knows that he can defeat us if he can get us looking only at what we can see or feel. This is the opposite of faith.

> *We walk by faith and not by sight.*
>
> 2 Corinthians 5:7

Faith is our response of trust and confidence in God's promises, which is what enables us to receive them. We receive everything God has for us by grace—what He has freely given us—through faith in Him, in His Word.

When we were believing for a healing miracle for our daughter, there were many times we had the opportunity to be gripped with negative emotions. The doctors' negative reports, bad test results, constantly dealing with hospitals, medication, pain, exhaustion, balancing the rest of the family's needs, and financial strain. All of these competed for our time and attention.

Hannah had an incurable autoimmune disease that meant her body could not digest protein, and at three years old she was the same size as a nine-month-old baby. The rare condition baffled the doctors, and at three and a half she was given a week to live.

Somewhere inside of me I knew that I must not allow my mind to entertain thoughts of her dying. We could not afford to focus on anything other than God's Word if we were to win the battle. Thoughts of Hannah dying were always there, but now I realize how important it was that we did not allow ourselves to dwell on them or else they would have carried us places we didn't want to go.

The biggest battle is that crazy fluff between our ears. However, the good news is that we can change the way we think and take captive those thoughts which are not from God.

> *Casting down arguments and every high thing that exalts itself against the knowledge of God, bringing every thought into captivity to the obedience of Christ.*
>
> 2 Corinthians 10:5

Jesus tells us that all things are possible to him who believes, and to *only* believe (Mark 9:23, Mark 5:36). That's good advice!

ALL IS NOT LOST

Looking back at Peter again, other than Jesus, he was the only recorded man to ever walk on water. He walked on top of the storm—the circumstances that said it was impossible and the thoughts that told him he was crazy—as long as he kept his focus on Jesus. He did not start to sink until he began to look away from Jesus and focus on the size of those circumstances!

Peter had to take control of those crazy thoughts in order to step out of the boat to begin with. Fear was real in the moment, but faith overcame it!

I have come to find that the more we step out and believe God for the impossible, the more crazy fluff there is to take captive, but the greater the victory is in the end!

Thought Traffic Control

Life happens, daily. People speak, act and change, governments rise and fall, life begins and ends, the weather changes drastically, traffic ebbs and flows—all outside of our control without our input or permission.

It is often those moments which we can't control that disturb our thoughts the most. Those are things that play over and over in our minds while we lay awake at night, wondering if we will see every hour tick 'round on the clock because we can't switch off our brains to sleep.

The truth is, we will never be able to control everything around us, but we can learn to control those thoughts that stride onto the battlefield of our mind like they own the place and send us spinning in circles. It is a position of strength to be able to sit back and realize, "This is not my circus, and those are not my monkeys!" Or, as King David said, "This battle belongs to the Lord!"

In that moment of surrender, we become the ringmaster in this circus called life! No longer is life pushing us about, but we step into the realm of authority in which God intended for us to live all along.

> In that moment of surrender, we become the ringmaster in this circus called life!

The importance of my ability to control my own thoughts was never more real to me than in those moments when life and death were hanging in the balance. When those who should have protected me betrayed my trust; when fear paralyzed my muscles until they became rigid; when disappointment was a given and hopelessness was normal; when thoughts of suicide hung over me and life seemed too painful to keep going.

And when I'd had so many seizures that I needed to learn to walk again; when the doctors told us that our unborn baby was deformed and offered us a termination; when our child was sent home from the hospital to die; when we were sued, and it looked like we would lose everything.

When life hurt so badly it was hard to breathe…It was in those times that our survival depended upon the ability to listen to the voice of God above the noise of the circus.

One day, the Lord showed me that I had power over my thoughts through a simple picture of an airport control tower with planes circling around it. Each time a plane approached the tower and came into radio contact, it had to request permission to land. Those planes did not have the authority to land without the go-ahead from the control tower.

Our thoughts are like those planes. We cannot stop those planes from coming into contact with our minds, but we do not have to give them permission to land!

This is what the Bible is talking about when it mentions taking every thought captive (2 Corinthians 10:3-5). We can literally recognize and isolate thoughts and judge whether they are good, bad, or ugly. In other words, are they from God, the devil, or just our flesh? A great way to decide this is John 10:10:

The thief cometh not but to steal and to kill and to destroy. I am come that they might have life, and that they might have it more abundantly.

Don't give negative thoughts permission to land!

Does the thought bring fear or dread? That would be from the enemy. Does it fill us with love, joy, peace? That would likely be God. The flesh can be a little harder to distinguish sometimes, but if we are seeking first the kingdom of God, chances are that our ambitions will be in line with His. Failing that, the Holy Spirit will guide us in the right direction because we are in relationship with Him.

In finding a thought circulating that's not good or God, serve the eviction notice! That would be anything that challenges a promise of God: fear, anger, poverty, sickness, despair, etc.

This amazing ability on the inside of every believer enables us to be in control of our emotions rather than having our emotions control us. Thoughts left unattended can quickly turn into a runaway herd of wild horses—they need training before they overrun the circus!

Thought Replacement

In order to change your thoughts, you can't just say, "Stop thinking about that!" For example, let's say I tell you, "Think of a fish." Your fish could be any number of species, with an infinite combination of shapes and colors. However, if I say, "Think of a purple fish with green stripes," a new picture will pop into your head.

Yet if we want to completely change the thought of a fish, I would need to redirect the picture in your mind completely. I might say something like, "Think of a snow-capped mountain, towering over a green valley filled with wildflowers."

Did you notice that the picture in your mind completely changed from the fish to the mountain vista?

We control our thoughts and emotions using this same tactic: by replacing negative thoughts and emotions with the Word of God!

Replace negative thoughts and emotions with the Word of God.

For example, rent is due this coming Friday, but you don't get your regular paycheck until *next* Friday. Many of us have faced this exact situation! Our natural minds might think, *Oh man, I won't get paid in time, and I don't even have close to the money I need to pay rent. What am I gonna do? Maybe our landlord will give us an extension. But I want to be faithful; I don't want to be late! I'm going to get evicted…Where will we go? I could ask my friend if we can stay with them for a while, but I don't want to impose. What if they say no? There isn't even enough room in our cars for all of us to sleep in there! Where will we shower? I don't want to be homeless!*

Wow, do you see how those thoughts went through expecting to not have money to pay rent, to imagining coping with homelessness? This is how the natural mind begins to rationalize our circumstances without any thought to what the Word of God says, even as a believer wanting to do the right thing. And these are the circles of thought that keep us anxiously awake at night!

We have to replace these thoughts with the promises of God, the Word of God, and visions and imaginations of what we are believing God to see!

Let's take the example above and replace those thoughts with the Word:

"Jesus, you said not to worry about our physical needs because our good Father God already knows that we need them. My paycheck is irrelevant in this situation, Lord, because You supply all of my needs according to Your riches in glory. I have favor with God, favor with man, and a good understanding. I ask You for wisdom with my finances, and I know that you are giving me that wisdom. Rent, you are paid, in Jesus' name! Lord, I don't know how You are going to pull this off, but I know You will! The how doesn't matter because I know the end result will be amazing. We will be in this home, with food to eat, no lack in our lives, and with an abundance to give to every good work. I am Yours, and I lack no good thing! You take care of my family. I cast this care upon You, right now. I put my trust in You, Lord, and I know You will never let me down. It is finished, in Jesus' name!"

Now you have replaced those negative imaginations of homelessness with the truth that God always comes through for you, He will never let you down, and that He has promised to even provide more than enough for you! You have also given Him free rein to resolve this challenge however He sees fit. You haven't placed Him in a box by demanding the how. For example, "Lord, I ask that you have a random stranger hand rent to me in the street!" Instead, you have just said, "Lord, I trust You to provide for our needs in the best way possible." His plans are so much better than anything you can dream up.

This is your life, your air space. You can start controlling the air traffic in it today. Deny negative thoughts permission to land and watch the transformation in your life that happens as a result!

Now to him who is able to do immeasurably more than all we ask or imagine, according to his power that is at work within us.

Ephesians 3:20

Refusing Defeat

Sometimes seeing the victory means refusing to see defeat. This was something that I realized shortly before moving to the United States, lying on my back in a grassy field! I had chased our cat across the farmyard in a vain attempt to rescue a baby rabbit that was dangling from its mouth, when my foot became lodged in a muddy rut under the grass. Momentum carried me past that hole, and I heard a loud crack originating from my ankle, which hadn't made the journey at the same speed as the rest of my body.

Sometimes seeing the victory means refusing to see defeat.

A half-mile from the house, all alone in the wet grass, I began to picture myself hobbling through the airport on crutches, dragging three small children and eighteen pieces of luggage toward the plane. We were in the middle of packing the house to move continent, and a broken ankle was not something that I had time for at that moment!

Suddenly, I had a choice to make. I could lie there and hope someone might hear me screaming, crawl back to the house across the field, and continue to imagine myself in a cast, or I could change the picture.

Because I had prepared myself by spending time in the Word of God and learning His promises, out of my mouth came a shout. It was my giant-killing battle cry, and all it said was, "Jesus!" I leapt to my feet and ran all the way home on a broken ankle. Yes, those first steps hurt—a lot—but by the time I got home, *my ankle was healed!*

I rejected the picture of myself hobbling through the airport on crutches and replaced it with an image of healing and victory. I'm not some super-duper Christian. The Word of God works, no matter who you are! If you will put your relationship with God first place, and use the Word to prepare yourself for victory, you can have the same results.

> *Finally, brethren, whatever things are true, whatever things are noble, whatever things are just, whatever things are pure, whatever things are lovely, whatever things are of good report, if there is any virtue and if there is anything praiseworthy—meditate on these things.*
>
> Philippians 4:8

If your thoughts aren't conforming to these guidelines in Philippians 4:8, it's time to change your perspective. What are you picturing? What does victory look like to you today, and what are you shouting at your giant? Take some time and reflect on the negative imaginations you have been having. Then deliberately research and find scriptures that will combat those thoughts. Begin to meditate on the positive and paint a new picture in your mind of success rather than failure.

Paint a picture in your mind of success.

Have those scriptures handy: carry them around with you on notecards, or in your smartphone. As you practice thought traffic control, you will find that seeing things from God's perspective becomes easier, your faith will grow, and you will see the impact as you begin to walk through life as a victor!

Fully Equipped

If we are to stand up to the enemy, we need to go out to battle properly dressed. Good armor is unique and custom made for the bearer. No one can wear your armor and you can't wear theirs. David found this out when Saul tried to clothe him in his armor to fight Goliath. David tried it on, but it was heavy and cumbersome. It didn't fit David's body, nor his fighting style (1 Samuel 17:38-39). He was an expert with a slingshot,

ALL IS NOT LOST

not with a sword. The armor he needed wasn't of the physical variety. David's armor was built from his faith in God, and that is what led him to victory over his giant.

In the same way, God has given us armor that fully equips us for our battles. It is designed specifically for us and is donned and used by faith.

> *Therefore take up the whole armor of God that you may be able to with stand in the evil day having done all to stand.*
>
> Ephesians 6:13

God has given us a whole suit of spiritual armor to protect us and equip us for life in the world. Many Christians are so overcome by the fact that they have their helmet of salvation that they fail to put on the rest of the armor—they are naked, streaking believers wearing just a helmet! What a picture!

Don't be a naked, streaking believer who is only wearing the helmet of salvation!

150

The armor of God is comprised of spiritual clothing rather than the tangible clothing we are accustomed to putting on every day. So, how do we actually dress ourselves in equipment that cannot be touched? These clothes are put on through faith, using our confession and imagination, fueled by our everyday relationship with God.

As His divine power has given to us all things that pertain to life and godliness, through the knowledge of Him...

2 Peter 1:3

Every benefit of our faith comes through relationship with God. As we know Him more and more, we can fully take part in every blessing He has given us, including the armor of God. Our trust in God—which can only be developed by spending time with Him—enables us to partake, take up, put on the armor of God and see the His promises working in our lives.

God is a spirit. Therefore, He communicates with us spirit to spirit. We hear His voice, and build our relationship with Him, spiritually. God gave us spiritual armor because we are in a spiritual battle. So, we need to know what our spiritual weapons are and how to use them spiritually.

Put on God's whole armor [the armor of a heavy-armed soldier which God supplies], that you may be able successfully to stand up against [all] the strategies and the deceits of the devil. For we are not wrestling

with flesh and blood [contending only with physi-
cal opponents], but against the despotisms, against
the powers, against [the master spirits who are] the
world rulers of this present darkness, against the
spirit forces of wickedness in the heavenly (supernat-
ural) sphere. Therefore put on God's complete armor,
that you may be able to resist and stand your ground
on the evil day [of danger], and, having done all
[the crisis demands], to stand [firmly in your place].
Stand therefore [hold your ground], having tightened
the belt of truth around your loins and having put
on the breastplate of integrity and of moral rectitude
and right standing with God, And having shod your
feet in preparation [to face the enemy with the firm-
footed stability, the promptness, and the readiness
produced by the good news] of the Gospel of peace.
Lift up over all the [covering] shield of saving faith,
upon which you can quench all the flaming missiles
of the wicked [one]. And take the helmet of salvation
and the sword that the Spirit wields, which is the
Word of God.

Ephesians 6:10-16 AMPC

Belt of Truth

Looking at the armor of God, it starts with the belt of truth.
Like David understood what he needed to battle Goliath, we

need to know the truth of who we really are first. The belt of truth is a belt off which all the other spiritual weapons hang; it is foundational to our armor.

The first piece of armor that a soldier wore was the belt. Centuries ago, men would wrestle with only a belt. The object of the match was to remove the opponent's belt. If satan can disarm us of our belt of truth, he will defeat us, for his greatest weapon is deceit. If we are under his control, it is because we have believed one of his lies instead of the truth of God's Word. Jesus said, "I am...the truth..." (John 14:6). To have the belt of truth on is to allow Jesus to lead the way, to have your eyes focused only on Him.

If we don't know the truth, we won't use it! In Bible days, men wore robes or gowns. When they fought or ran, they had to gird up their loins; they would reach down for the back of their robes, pull it up through to the front and tuck the end into their belt. Elijah did this to outrun a horse-drawn chariot in 2 Kings.

Fist Peter 1:3 tells us to gird up the loins of our minds! In other words, watch your thoughts and speech. Therefore, Paul is saying that truth is the belt that allows us to fight without being entangled in our garments. Those who do not surround themselves with truth will become entangled in their own web of deceit and will fall. Just because a lie is repeated often enough that people begin to believe it, it doesn't make it truth.

Growing up in a positive environment, children tend to mature into secure and confident adults. On the other hand, negative influences on a consistent basis produce insecurity, and instability. The good news is that the Word of God will work for anyone, regardless of how they were raised, what they have done, or where they were born. If today you see yourself as someone struggling with identity, lacking confidence, low self-esteem, or insecurity, you are the ideal candidate for Holy Spirit transformation!

You are the ideal candidate for Holy Spirit transformation!

Breastplate of Righteousness

Our breastplate of righteousness protects our hearts. When the Bible refers to the heart, it is often referring to the soul: the mind, will and emotions.

When we became born again, our spirits became righteous. We are the righteousness of God in Christ (2 Corinthians 5:17). Our right standing with God through Jesus is the foundation of our relationship with our Father. Therefore, our hearts need protection, and they are protected when we understand and believe that we have been made righteous through faith in Jesus.

If satan can make us believe we have to earn our right-standing with God, he can get us into self-righteousness—trying to earn the right to fellowship with God. And self-righteousness results in weak, distracted, ineffective Christians because we are relying on our own strength and behavior rather than on the gift of righteousness we have received through Jesus!

> *So above all, guard the affections of your heart, for they affect all that you are. Pay attention to the welfare of your innermost being, for from there flows the wellspring of life.*
>
> Proverbs 4:23 TPT

The affections of our hearts—what we listen to, think upon, act upon, repeat to others, what we believe about ourselves—impact everything about us.

The NKJV translation puts it this way:

> *Keep your heart with all diligence, for out of it spring the issues of life.*

To "keep" means to place a guard over or set watch, like putting a shield over our heart to protect it or setting a guard to keep watch and protect it from intruders. If we don't protect our hearts from negative influences around us, it will do what it is designed to do: absorb everything around it and, from that information, form the very principles and moral values by which we live our lives.

The word *issues* means borders or boundaries. Out of our hearts are formed the boundaries or borders of our lives. If our hearts are full of things other than the truth of God's Word, we will form our own version of truth.

Human truth rather than Godly truth is based on experience, knowledge, opinion, the popular vote, or something else other than the Word of God. Spiritual dysfunction shows up in lives in the form of sickness, poverty, debt, chaos, broken relationships, mental health problems, addictions, perfectionism, emotional immaturity, insecurity...you have probably seen all of these at some point!

However, when we don the breastplate of righteousness, we can see that Jesus has already made us righteous! This weakens insecurity and gives us faith in our righteousness in Christ. When the enemy attacks us with thoughts of condemnation and dysfunction, trying to do damage to our hearts, the breastplate of our righteousness protects our hearts from these attacks! We can confidently go into battle, knowing that our victory is not based on our own actions, but on our faith in what Jesus has already done.

Feet Shod with Good News

The Gospel of Jesus Christ is good news! Ephesians 6:15 says, *"And having shod your feet with the **preparation** of the gospel of peace"* (emphasis added). We prepare for the way in which we will walk with the Word of God!

Jesus was the Word made flesh (John 1:14), and He is the Prince of Peace. When we prepare ourselves by renewing our minds to the Word of God and learning the fullness of the Gospel, we will have peace no matter where we go.

The reason the illustration of shoes is used in reference to the Gospel—the Word of God—is because it is what we stand on! It is the foundation of our faith. Everywhere we go, our path has been prepared by the Gospel, and we can walk in peace

How beautiful upon the mountains Are the feet of him who brings good news, Who proclaims peace, Who brings glad tidings of good things, Who proclaims salvation, Who says to Zion, "Your God reigns!"

Isaiah 52:7

The Word of God is
what we stand on!

Shield of Faith

The shield of faith is a part of our armor that is used for both defense and offense. Faith is powerful and it is what enables us to overcome the world (1 John 5:4). Defensively, our faith acts like a fire extinguisher and quenches all the fiery darts of the evil one. We can also use our faith to attack the enemy and make him flee (James 4:7).

By faith we move the promises of God from the spiritual world into the physical. It is our ability to act on God's Word and access the promises of God that His grace has provided to us (Romans 5:2). Through every storm or attack in this life, we walk in victory to the level that we put our trust in God.

Helmet of Salvation

The helmet of salvation protects the head. Understanding the security of our salvation is what protects our minds from lies of the enemy regarding our identity in Christ. When we become born-again, we are made completely righteous because of what Jesus has done for us. Knowing that our salvation is not easily lost keeps us from falling into deception. We know we are in right-standing with God, that He loves us unconditionally, and that His promises are not dependent upon our behavior.

Because our heads are protected, this gives us the confidence and authority to take our thoughts captive and harness our emotions. This is important because our emotions follow our thoughts, and our actions follow our emotions. Everything we feel, say, and do flows from our thoughts! Therefore, it is vital that we put on the helmet of salvation, acknowledging our proper position as righteous children of God.

Sword of the Spirit

The sword of the Spirit is the Word of God! This is our primary offensive weapon against the attacks of the enemy and circumstances of the fallen world in which we live. I can't underestimate the importance of the words that we speak. They are powerful! They become even more powerful when they come directly from the Word of God.

> *Death and life are in the power of the tongue, and those who love it will eat its fruit.*
>
> Proverbs 18:21

> *For the word of God is living and powerful, and sharper than any two-edged sword, piercing even to the division of soul and spirit, and of joints and marrow, and is a discerner of the thoughts and intents of the heart.*
>
> Hebrews 4:12

We have been given the most powerful and effective weapon God could possibly have equipped us with: His words! The

Bible is filled with the words of God, and He has given us the authority to use them in His name here on Earth. Using the sword of the Spirit—the Word of God—effectively is how we can live victoriously!

We have been given the most powerful and effective weapon God could possibly have equipped us with: His words!

Chapter Ten

The Power of Relationship

Faith is a powerful force—it overcomes the world. Faith lives inside in the person of Jesus but without love it doesn't function. Galatians 5:6 says that faith works by love. It is only by receiving the love of God, and allowing Him to love us, that we can begin to build in our hearts a picture of who we truly are.

[For my determined purpose is] that I may know Him [that I may progressively become more deeply and intimately acquainted with Him, perceiving and recognizing and understanding the wonders of His Person more strongly and more clearly], and that I may in that same way come to know the power outflowing from His resurrection [which it exerts over believers], and that I may so share His sufferings as to be continually transformed [in spirit into His likeness even] to His death, [in the hope] That if possible I may attain to the [spiritual and moral] resurrection

[that lifts me] out from among the dead [even while in the body]. Not that I have now attained [this ideal], or have already been made perfect, but I press on to lay hold of (grasp) and make my own, that for which Christ Jesus (the Messiah) has laid hold of me and made me His own.

Philippians 3:10-12 AMPC

We were created to be in relationship with God, and through that relationship the miraculous power of God flows. Jesus is in our DNA, we were made in His image, given His name and authority. The dictionary defines the word *dysfunctional* as "a person or thing that is not operating properly." Life without God is dysfunctional, it just doesn't work right.

So, how do we begin to guard what goes into our heart and develop healthy boundaries that are based in God's truth, and function as God intended us to?

When technology goes bad (the computer gets a virus or bug or just gets sluggish in its responses) we reset it, restore it to the default or factory settings so that it can operate as it was intended to when it was first created.

Take a look at our default settings. This is usually our first response; it is what comes out when we are under pressure. These pressure responses to life circumstances are often pure emotion: fear, anger, insecurity, worry, disappointment, or confusion and result in negative outcomes. Praise Jesus that we don't have to stay stuck there!

Firstly, just like smacking a computer with a hammer won't fix it (I have felt like doing this frequently), beating ourselves up doesn't work real well either. Everyone has a level of dysfunction in their lives, no matter how well put together they may appear, so don't fall for the enemy's condemnation trick. He is the accuser of the brethren, so, that's just him doing his job. Anytime he tries bringing up my past mistakes, I like to personally remind him of his future—I've read the end of the book, and we win!

Secondly, with any malfunctioning techie item, the standard response is to check if it's plugged in. Yes, I may have once or twice failed to recognize that the power source was not connected. Being connected to the power source is vital for functionality, and this is true in our relationship with God as well. If we want to see the power of God flow through us, lift us up out of our pit, heal our hearts, find our purpose, and empower us to live the kind of lives He always had for us, we have to be plugged in.

Being connected to the power source is vital for functionality.

ALL IS NOT LOST

> *...that I may know Him and the power of His resurrection...*
>
> Philippians 3:10

The word *know* in this scripture is not talking about a casual meeting like we just started chatting to a stranger on the bus. It's describing an intimate relationship, like in a marriage. We can't experience the benefits and intimacy of marriage if we settle for a one-night stand relationship with Jesus! Relationships take quality and quantity time where we learn about each other. The more we learn about someone, the better we "know" them, and the easier it is to spot a lie.

Spiritual Small Talk

Spending time getting to really know the Lord is what I call spiritual small talk. It may sound weird to you, but I have conversations with Jesus. He is a real person with thoughts, opinions, ideas, and a great sense of humor. If you don't think God has a sense of humor you have obviously never seen a duck-billed platypus!

How do you have a conversation with God? The same way you do with a physical person. If you want to hear what the other person has to say, you need to come up for air now and then. Sometimes our prayer life is all talking, and we wonder why we are struggling to hear God speak.

Likewise, if all we do is hit up God in our crisis moments, that makes for a poor relationship. Our Father loves to help us through the crisis moments but there is so much more to our relationship with Him than we realize—we will need all of eternity to experience it.

By spending time getting to know the Lord, listening to His voice, and focusing our thoughts to be more in line with His, we will start to see breakthrough—effectively we are restoring our factory settings!

What we have as our foundation of truth will no longer be in the ideals of the world but based upon God's Word. This is the truth that sets us free and the foundation upon which the weapons of our warfare hang.

Sometimes our prayer life is all talking, and we wonder why we are struggling to hear God speak.

Hearing God's Voice

We are God's children! He wants to be in an active relationship with us: to talk to us, position us, keep us from harm, lead us into open doors of opportunity and success, and speak healing, deliverance, and prosperity into our lives.

If you are a child of God, you *can* hear His voice! The enemy would like nothing more than to convince you that you are unable to hear God because he knows just what you are capable of when you know you've got a word from God. I hear people often say, "I can't hear God speaking to me. I try to listen, but I just can't hear him!" This is a lie of the enemy. As long as you believe you cannot hear God's voice, you will be unable to hear Him. Instead, choose to believe what the Word says about you:

He who is of God hears God's words...

John 8:47

My sheep hear My voice, and I know them, and they follow Me.

John 10:27

As long as you believe you cannot hear God's voice, you will be unable to hear Him.

If the devil can convince you that you are unable to hear God (which is a lie), then you won't truly be able to listen to hear God's voice speak to you. And if you aren't listening—if you haven't trained your heart to recognize when He is speaking—His ability to work good in your life will be limited.

The Cat Is Eating Your Pie

In a farmhouse long ago, on a rainy afternoon, I decided to bake a pie. It doesn't sound particularly spiritual, but everyone was out and about, and I had a rare moment of alone time to do something creative. So, the pie baking commenced and filled the house with glorious odors of yumminess. I set the pie on top of the stove to cool while I sat down to check emails. Our three farm cats, aka the mousers, assembled themselves around me to stare at the moving images on the computer screen and periodically trample across my keyboard.

In my journey with Jesus, I had recently discovered that small talk was as equally important with Him as it was in any earthly relationship. Hearing God in the little things, learning to tune in to His still small voice for direction, and following it was vital. Sometimes life got busy, and taking time to develop spiritual listening ears was a new adventure.

However, as I pecked away at the keyboard that afternoon, the last thing that I thought I would hear the Lord say was, "The cat is eating your pie!" It sounded so off the wall that I did what most people do and ignored it, thinking that it was a result of eating too much cheese.

The three cats were sitting next to me, all present and certainly not eating my pie. After the third time, the thought on the inside of me was so loud in my head that I looked around me at the cats and decided that I had to go and get a visual of my pie anyway, just to be safe.

As I headed into the kitchen, there on the stovetop was a cat—eating my pie! Greater than the shock of a strange cat finding its way into my kitchen and eating my pie, was the fact that God, the Creator of the universe, was so in tune with my life that He would take the time to speak to me about a pie and that I could hear Him!

The truth is that we can all hear Him, all of the time. He is constantly thinking about us and talking to us. We just need to be ready to listen.

God is constantly thinking about us and talking to us.

The Importance of Hearing God's Voice

It is important to hear God's voice for many reasons, but mostly because He knows the way ahead. He knows us, our past, our future, and the path that will most fulfill our hopes and dreams. The Holy Spirit leads us into truth, shows a way of escape in times of danger, reveals our future and purpose, convicts and teaches us, opens doors of opportunity for us, and loves us with an everlasting love. In fact, hearing God's voice can be a life-or-death situation!

This ability to hear God was made more real to me that day, but I didn't realize how important that would prove to be until a few days later. I was driving down the hedge-lined country lane taking our children to school, when I heard inside of me, "Brake!!"

I didn't question it: I immediately stomped on the brake without thinking. Out of a hidden farm gate in front of me shot another vehicle! We would have collided head-on at 60 mph if I had not stopped when I did. Listening to the Lord that day probably saved our lives.

Take time today to hang out with Jesus. Talk about the little things! Small talk is a powerful part of developing an intimate relationship. It is amazing what we will hear when we take time to listen.

Be still and know that I am God.

Psalm 46:10

The Hitchhiker

My husband has a story of his own regarding the life-or-death importance of hearing God's voice, but I'll let him tell it:

> One day, I was driving, and I saw a hitchhiker walking down the side of the road. I heard the still, small voice of the Lord say, "Pick up that hitchhiker." At first, I thought, *No, that's just me,* because I really didn't want to! In fact, I even passed him by. But after I had passed, it was like the Holy Spirit was yelling at me to pick him up! So, I made a U-turn and went back for him.
>
> After we started driving, he asked me, "So, what do you do for a living?"
>
> I answered, "I'm a minister."
>
> He looked at me and said, "Are you kidding me? Just two minutes ago I prayed, and I said, 'God, send someone to help me. I need one of your workers to help me!'"
>
> We spent about 20 minutes together. He had been born again years ago, but that day in the truck, he rededicated his life to the Lord. I also led him in the baptism of the Holy Spirit, and he received his prayer language. It was a powerful time of ministry!
>
> When I dropped him off, he got out of my truck and said, "I want you to know, this was going to be my last night. I was going to end everything

THE POWER OF RELATIONSHIP

tonight. I prayed today, and I said, 'God, if You love me, You're going to have to show me.' And spending time with you today has really encouraged me—I feel like a new man now!"

He had started off beaten down and considering suicide, but he left encouraged and ready go live life!

God's Got This!

Moving to another country is a mammoth undertaking of epic proportions. No matter which way we looked at it, hauling three small children and 18 pieces of luggage (most of those filled with Legos) thousands of miles to a country we had never visited—without any backup plan, place to live, or transportation (other than a one-way plane ticket)—appeared (to any ordinary human being) just a tad irresponsible. Except for the fact that we were not then—and still aren't now—ordinary human beings!

Our journey across the ocean began with a quiet stirring on the inside that we came to recognize was God. The simple, wild idea grew legs as we discussed it, and then it developed into us applying for a visa. Against all odds, including the US Embassy, God made a way for us to step into the plans He had for us. Knowing that He was making straight the paths ahead—in ways that only He could—gave us the confidence to take the plunge and charter a course into the unknown.

After living in America for several years, it became time to apply for our permanent resident status or green card. Unsuccessful applications result in applicants having just a matter of weeks to leave the country. By this point, our kids were well settled and barely remembered life back home. What they knew was home to them. But our application was complicated and selected for review at least six times! It didn't look good.

It was during this long, and stressful, process—when the mountain appeared so huge that it looked like it would fall on us—that God reminded me of something. This adventure was His idea, not mine. This was subtle at first, and momentarily comforting, but soon I was busy fixing the problems and addressing each challenge as it came, on my own.

I got this, I thought. Yeah, well that didn't go too well for me, and I was far from chill! From somewhere near the bottom of the paperwork pile, I waved my white flag! If all else fails, seek the Lord, right?!

So, what did the Lord say? He showed me a picture of an army, thousands strong, lined up facing me across a valley. To my left and right stood my army, all on horseback ready to charge but hopelessly outnumbered. Every one of them looked at me to give them instruction, depending on me to lead them to victory. No pressure, right?! As I wondered how anything good might come of this battle, He asked me a question: "Do you want to know what your horse's name is?"

What kind of question is that at a time like this? I thought. Then it came to me: my horse's name was Holy Spirit! We couldn't both be leading the charge. In order to win that battle, I knew that I needed to let go of the reins. As they fell from my hands, Holy Spirit began to move toward the army, and one by one every opponent fell away, until none remained. The moment I let go, God won the battle!

> The moment I let go of the reins,
> God won the battle!

Now thanks be to God who always leads us in triumph in Christ, and through us diffuses the fragrance of His knowledge in every place.

2 Corinthians 2:14

You are of God, little children, and have overcome them, because He who is in you is greater than he who is in the world.

1 John 4:4

We received a letter informing us that we had been randomly selected for a special investigation by the U.S. immigration department. During the coming interview, we were informed that our three young children would be separated from us for questioning. As a parent, this idea was horrifying!

However, we knew that the Lord had told us to come to America and we had followed Him all along this journey. Even though we were faced with our children being separated from us in this investigation, and the potential consequences of being uprooted and sent back to England, the Lord reminded us that He is trustworthy, and we could have confidence in Him. He told us, "Don't worry about it. This is just a formality."

The day of our interview, we were prepared for a long wait and braced for the separation and interviews. However, after around ten minutes, an officer came to greet us. He said, "Oh, Terradez family! You know what, you can all come in together. This won't take but a minute. Don't worry, **this is just a formality!**" The entire process took about twenty minutes: it was supernatural!

When we experience negative circumstances, the flesh naturally begins to look at those things that can be seen and felt. However, the things we verify with our five senses are only temporary; the things we have already been given by God are eternal (2 Corinthians 4:18). To overcome these bumps in the road—for our faith to effectively access the grace of God—we must instead focus on every good thing that is in us in Christ Jesus!

Circumstances are irrelevant to God's ability to fulfill His plans! God is the only one in charge, regardless of what the natural, or "normal" expectations might be. Even when people come against you, or the devil, they cannot stop the promises of God from coming to pass in your life.

Circumstances are irrelevant to God's ability to fulfill His plans!

The only person who can limit the Word of God, and His plans for your life, is you. We build the barriers and limitations in our minds based on previous experiences, human knowledge or probability. Those limitations shatter as you acknowledge all of the promises of God—every good thing that is already in you!

Learning to Hear God's Voice

God is always speaking to us. It's as though He is transmitting on a radio station at a specific frequency, and we have to tune in to that particular wavelength to hear Him clearly. Perhaps sometimes we are not quite there, so the signal seems clouded with static. The dial needs to be adjusted just a little to get the clearest sound. Once we do, and we are hearing God's voice, we still have to be willing to take a step of faith and follow!

Sometimes it may be to pick up a hitchhiker, but sometimes it may be to *not* pick them up! It could be saying to move to another country, or that a cat is eating your pie. We must practice hearing His voice and acting on what He tells us to do because our lives, or the lives of others, may depend on it. So, how do we learn to tune in to His broadcast?

The short answer is that we have to develop our relationship with God. We just have to know Him more and more! Married couples will tell you that after years of marriage they can predict exactly how their spouse would react in any given situation. The more you know God's nature—who He truly is—the easier it is to recognize His voice. He will never violate His nature or His Word, so the more intimate you become with who He is, the easier it is to discard thoughts or voices that want to lead you away from His plan.

There are a few basic principles that will help you to become more sensitive to the voice of God.

1. The voice of God will never contradict scripture. If you hear something that is contrary to His Word, it is not Him! The more familiar you are with the Scriptures, the easier hearing God's voice will become.

2. Understand that God will never lead you through paralyzing or tormenting fear. This fear is different from the fear of the Lord, which is reverence or awe of God—a respect for His leading. If anything brings you to a place of anxiety or panic, it is

usually either not Him, or your flesh flashing! Give it over to prayer and allow the peace of God to rule in your heart (Colossians 3:15).

3. Believe and confess that you *do* hear God's voice. Refuse to submit to the lie of the enemy that you can't hear God. John 10:27 says that you can!

4. Spend time with God. As you do this, you'll become more intimate with Him and more easily able to determine His heart and motivations.

5. Be obedient. When you have heard His voice, don't rely on logic, just obey! Sometimes you may make mistakes, but as you take action in response, you will become more sensitive to His leading and understand Him more clearly.

6. Don't limit God. Sometimes we only give God a couple of choices, when His plan includes so much more! Be open to His leading in situations you may be facing. He can make a way where there seems to be no way!

Expect to hear from God today! He is not hiding from you: He loves you and is always speaking. His desire is for you to always hear Him clearly.

Chapter Eleven

Comeback Keys

There are two keys the Lord showed me that I remember anytime life presents me with opportunity to feel like all is lost. These have helped me keep focused on the finish line rather than the hurdle ahead, and to trust God to deliver me in the midst of adversity. Ultimately, these keys set me back on track when I need help to overcome.

Three Days Can Change Everything

Jesus was celebrated, paraded as a king through the streets on a donkey, and honored. Yet this was short-lived, because soon after, He was crucified.

This was not how His disciples thought it was going to end. In their minds, Jesus was going to set up a physical kingdom here on Earth and rule as the King of the Jews. Despite Jesus foretelling His death, and the coming of the Holy Spirit to comfort and guide them, they didn't get it.

"I still have many things to say to you, but you cannot bear them now. However, when He, the Spirit of truth, has come, He will guide you into all truth; for He will not speak on His own authority, but whatever He hears He will speak; and He will tell you things to come. He will glorify Me, for He will take of what is Mine and declare it to you. All things that the Father has are Mine. Therefore I said that He will take of Mine and declare it to you. A little while, and you will not see Me; and again a little while, and you will see Me, because I go to the Father." Then some of His disciples said among themselves, "What is this that He says to us, 'A little while, and you will not see Me; and again a little while, and you will see Me'; and, 'because I go to the Father'?" They said therefore, "What is this that He says, 'A little while'? We do not know what He is saying."

John 16:12-18

At the crucifixion, it looked to the disciples like all was lost and the devil had won. They didn't know that three days later Jesus would rise from the dead and change the course of history forever. They witnessed the man they loved—who they had followed for three years, for whom they had given up families, businesses, friends, and reputations—brutally crucified. Their hopes and expectations crushed, their own lives now in danger, they huddled together in fear and prayed.

As they gathered behind the locked door, suddenly Jesus appeared right there in the midst of them—all cool, like He hadn't just walked through a wall—and said a phrase they would instantly recognize, "Peace be with you" (John 20:19).

All was not lost: it was the just the beginning for them! The first day of the rest of their lives had just begun, and it started with peace.

Jesus was not just throwing out there some simple greeting or telling them to chill out because maybe they thought they had seen a ghost again. He isn't called the Prince of Peace for no reason!

Peace is a force to be reckoned with. It is the resting pulse rate of every faith-filled believer. Peace is the power twin of faith. It was the culmination of everything Jesus had just spent the past few days accomplishing while in the grave, and the future legacy of everything He had deposited inside those who love Him.

Peace is a force to be reckoned with. It is the power twin of faith.

Peace in the Hebrew language of the Old Testament is *shalom*. It means much more than just rest or calm. It is safety, rest, health, happiness, wholeness, prosperity, favor, and friendship.

> *He is despised and rejected by men, A Man of sorrows and acquainted with grief. And we hid, as it were, our faces from Him; He was despised, and we did not esteem Him. Surely He has borne our griefs And carried our sorrows; Yet we esteemed Him stricken, Smitten by God, and afflicted. But He was wounded for our transgressions, He was bruised for our iniquities; The chastisement for our peace was upon Him, And by His stripes we are healed. All we like sheep have gone astray; We have turned, every one, to his own way; And the Lord has laid on Him the iniquity of us all.*
>
> Isaiah 53:3-6

Jesus was prophesied by Isaiah as the arm of the Lord who would be despised and rejected by men, a man who would feel and carry our sorrow, pain and grief, our sickness and disease, our anxiety and worry. He physically took away these things from us by making the payment for our sin. The entire weight of every hurt, every pain, every loss that we would encounter was carried by Jesus on the cross.

They were defeated in that moment so that we could live in His peace, His safety, His healing, His provision, His favor, His rest, and experience a happiness and friendship that only comes through relationship with Him. All this was accomplished before we were even born, before we were capable of loving or serving Him.

This is the peace that Jesus left as an inheritance before He died—the peace He told the disciples would carry them through and keep them from fear in the time to come.

> *Peace I leave with you, My peace I give to you; not as the world gives do I give to you. Let not your heart be troubled, neither let it be afraid.*
>
> John 14:27

This wasn't just any restful sentiment. Jesus said, "*MY* peace I give to you." His very own Peace. The Passion Translation puts it this way:

> *I leave the gift of peace with you—my peace. Not the kind of fragile peace given by the world, but my perfect peace...*

Peace is the word spoken to the storm that threatened to shipwreck the disciples. It contained enough power to calm the storm and reset the situation (Mark 4:39).

Our confidence has to be in God alone, not in the circumstances or even others around us. People fail, even with the best intentions, but God is always on our side.

> *You will keep him in perfect peace, Whose mind is stayed on You, Because he trusts in You.*
>
> Isaiah 26:3

People fail, even with the best intentions, but God is always on our side.

No matter what is going on in your life, keep your eyes on Jesus! Whatever the situation, however bad it looks today, wait three days and it will look different. Responding hastily, out of reflex or fear, causes a bigger mess. Time helps us see things in perspective. It allows us to refocus on the Lord and hear Him above the noise of the storm, all while the Lord is intervening on our behalf. I have seen situations that appeared hopeless completely turn around as I took time to seek God rather than respond in the flesh!

God Can Handle Our Emotions

In times of tragedy, betrayal, confusion, helplessness, or just pure emotion, we do not think clearly. Our decisions are not always the best ones as we struggle to be objective. In those moments of whirling thoughts, the Holy Spirit is our Comforter. He is our voice of reason, our guide, our protection, our best friend. He alone can heal broken hearts, show us how to love our enemies and what forgiveness really looks like, but we have to participate.

Ultimately, we are the ones who hurt the most when we hold on to hurt, anger, pain, and unforgiveness, not the person who wronged us. These things become like a cancer in our bodies and will spread to other areas of life if we don't deal with them. So how do we deal with these feelings? How do we stop feeling them?

This is what works for me: I see a box, and in it I place all of the emotion—the thoughts, the confusion, the drama, the whole situation—in that box. I close the lid and address it to Jesus. In my mind, I mail it. I ask the Holy Spirit to be my comforter, and I place my trust in Him.

This is casting my cares upon the Lord! If at any time I begin to dwell on those thoughts and start to feel that hurt rising up inside of me, or fear creeping back, I picture that box again. I remember that those feelings are no longer mine to deal with; I already gave them to Jesus, so I refuse to take them back.

> *Be anxious for nothing, but in everything by prayer and supplication, with thanksgiving, let your requests be made known to God; and the peace of God, which surpasses all understanding, will guard your hearts and minds through Christ Jesus.*
>
> Philippians 4:6-7

Jesus is the original comeback King, and He lives in us. Jesus in us is greater than any obstacle; He always leads us to victory and causes us to triumph (2 Corinthians 2:14). Be encouraged today that you have everything you need inside of you to be who He called you to be. And if that devil tries to send any of his junk your way, just label it, "Return to Sender!"

Decision Time

When I see a promise in the Word of God, or when He specifically directs me and shows me things to come, my strong-willed, childlike tenacity kicks in. There are some things that are worth fighting for. We naturally would fight to protect our loved ones from harm, we would speak up against false accusations, we'd advocate for the helpless, we would stand in the gap for someone else if the occasion demanded it. But what about ourselves? When the enemy comes with his lies, deceit and accusations trying to undermine what God has told us belongs to us, do we stand up then? Or do we hand over our peace, hang our heads in shame, and figure it was all too good to be true?

A few years ago, I found myself at a point of decision. Was I going to hold on to the word God had spoken to me, or was I going to confess every negative thought, all manner of feelings and play the pity party card? Actually, I kind of did a little of everything!

Two years prior, I had had a vision of our whole family, all five of us, standing on a beach in Australia taking pictures. I knew that God was going to open up a door for us to minister there and powerful miracles would take place. Sure enough, two years later we were on our way. The cases were packed, checked in and on their way to Brisbane. We, however, got hung up in LAX. Not my favorite airport—it's huge, busy, and always under construction. After a delay, we headed to the gate for our final long leg, only to discover that my husband's visa was not electronically attached to his passport.

He was not allowed to board the plane.

Now, the schedule of meetings planned for us was intense. We would be landing the following morning at five in the morning to start preaching at noon. With two of us sharing the teaching, we could make it work. We had been told that people were flying in from all over Australia just for our conference. Yet, it was ten in the evening, the Australian embassy was closed, and Ashley was not allowed on the plane.

The best we could do was to have me fly on as planned and have Ashley join me later. It was super late, I was very tired, very emotional, and definitely not displaying my finest qualities. I boarded the plane last, along with our two boys, while Ashley and Hannah stayed behind at LAX. My face on that plane was one of "Don't talk to me, don't touch me, I might just lose it."

Our seats had been messed up, and we were squashed in the last economy row that didn't recline properly on a fifteen-hour flight to a place my flesh didn't want to go, without my husband—who ironically was the one who had planned this crazy schedule—and now I'd have to preach all *his* sessions *plus* mine with no sleep, not to mention pick up a rental car and drive stick shift for two hours on the wrong side of the road in a foreign county.

It was a bad day.

As the hours dragged by, my emotions collected, and the Lord and I began to talk. This trip was His idea. It was the fulfillment of a word that He gave me. The five of us would be there in Australia, and miracles would happen. As I reminded the Lord, in case He had forgotten, of how this whole thing came about, I noticed His silence. Then it hit me—His word was still good; it hadn't changed.

My whole attitude snapped to attention. I rooted my faith on those words, joined my confession to them, and said, "Lord, I need You to send someone to help me."

The flight landed, and we were met by two timid airline personnel at baggage claim—not a good sign, I thought. They broke the news to us that in the mix-up with the visa at LAX, the wrong bags had been removed from the aircraft. I had my husband's clothes in Brisbane, and he had mine and one of our boys' clothes back in LAX.

Awesome, I thought. *I guess we will need to go shopping before I preach in a few hours!* Rushing from the airport to the store, to the apartment to shower, and finally to the conference venue, we made it just in time. I had settled in my heart that this was not my problem to fix. We had moved on a word from God, ran into some opposition, requested divine intervention, and now my mind needed to be focused on those for whom I'd come.

Crossing the lobby area on the way to the meeting room, a lady approached me and introduced herself.

"You must be Carlie! But where is your husband?" she asked.

I explained the visa delay to which she responded, "I flew here to the conference from Sydney. I'm an immigration agent, and I'm the one—I'm here to help you!"

This lady, directed by the Lord, hopped on a plane herself to be there in person just to help us. Within a couple of days, Ashley arrived in Brisbane. He joined me at the conference, we saw many miracles, and yes, we took pictures on the beach with all five of us!

I learned an important lesson. In the face of adversity, we have to decide to win. To stand on the Word of God and not waver from it. It's what we do in the trial before we see the other side that determines the outcome. There is nothing comfortable in the moment between when God says, "Yes," and we say, "Amen." It feels like an eternity when all your flesh wants to throw a fit and your five senses are reporting every reason why victory is unlikely. Going against your flesh isn't natural or logical. It's a supernatural decision.

> *For to be carnally minded is death, but to be spiritually minded is life and peace.*
>
> Romans 8:6

In the face of adversity,
we have to decide to win.

Strengthen Yourself in the Lord

What we decide when under pressure tells us a lot about where our faith is at. During our return flight, I read through the story of King David and his battle at Ziklag (1 Samuel 30). David and his men had been away fighting battles for the Lord, and they were on their way home, probably looking forward to a home-cooked meal and their own beds. Upon their return to Ziklag, they didn't find the usual welcome. In fact, their city had been destroyed by the Amalekites and all of their wives and children taken captive.

David and his men were so distraught that they wept until there were no more tears left. So upset were the men, that they blamed David and threatened to stone him.

> *Now David was greatly distressed, for the people spoke of stoning him, because the soul of all the people was grieved, every man for his sons and his daughters. But David strengthened himself in the Lord his God.*
>
> 1 Samuel 30:6

David was distressed and in grief, not knowing what had happened to his family and having literally lost everything. He did the one thing under pressure that he knew to do—he strengthened himself in the Lord. Now, it doesn't tell us what that looked like, but knowing David, there would have been prayer, and praise and worship, all the things his flesh didn't feel like doing.

The word *strengthened* in this verse is *chazaq*. It means to seize, to fortify, to grow strong and cure, to hold strongly with, to man up, be courageous, and to conquer. He took emotional refuge in the Lord and found the courage and strength to see the victory on the other side of this battle. His attitude affected those around him, and with the power of God they went and recovered all that the enemy had stolen from them, and more. The Lord is on our side, and He is in the restoration business!

> The Lord is on our side, and He is in the restoration business!

I needed to remind myself of this when, on the way home from Australia, we landed at Denver airport, only to find that the very same suitcase which had gone missing on the way out had also gone missing again on the way home. The devil must

have really wanted to get his hands on my luggage! After waiting several hours and completing all the lost luggage forms, we
went home to wait for the airline to locate my bag and deliver
it to our house.

The next day, my bag still had not arrived, so I called and
spoke to the representative. She recommended I complete
an insurance form to claim compensation for all of my lost
belongings.

"Oh, no," I replied. "My suitcase is blessed, and it is coming back to me with nothing missing and nothing broken. I
have a word from God, and that suitcase will be returned.
I will recover all. I'm believing God, can I get your agree-
ment?" She didn't quite know how to respond, but she agreed
with me.

Of course, all that day, thoughts came to me, *You're never
getting that bag back. All those gifts you bought in Australia are
lost and you can't replace them. It's all lost.* My response was,
"Shut up, flesh!"

Well, the following day, we were out shopping for groceries
and Ashley received a call from an unknown Denver number.
We figured we should answer because it could have been the
baggage desk. However, it wasn't the airline. The caller was a
total stranger to us. He asked us if we had lost a bag, and if so,
could we describe it to him.

We described the bag, and this man had my suitcase! He
went on to tell us the incredible story of how it came to be in
his possession.

"Well," he said, "I was just cycling along this trail about forty-five minutes north of the city, out in the middle of nowhere. I noticed a black case sticking out from under a bush. I recognized it immediately as a suitcase because I was a baggage handler twenty-three years before I retired."

He had found my bag on a country bicycle path so far from a road that he had to get help to bring it back to his truck—how it got there, *only God knows!* Also, this baggage handler found my case and returned it to the lost luggage office of the same airline for which he had worked! And who else but a baggage handler would be brave enough to drag a suitcase out from under a bush in a remote location, having no idea what might be in it? Creepy!

The airline representative called me back after my bag arrived at her desk, a little muddy from its adventure.

"I don't know how to explain this," she said, "but your prayers worked!"

When I finally opened up that case, all of the contents were exactly as I'd packed them, untouched. I had recovered all that was lost!

Conclusion

All is not lost. It is just the beginning. The beginning of what? Your path from trauma, discouragement, and overwhelming obstacles to victory! This is a journey of faith, a path to freedom, the road to recovery, the discovery of who you really are, of who God called you to be, of your victory, your finest moment when you see how God can take your darkest times and make them His most glorious victories.

This doesn't happen overnight, but your path to wholeness and victory begins today. Recognize that even though yours may seem to be the most dramatic of underdog stories, you can emerge the victor!

There may be a process in discovering your true identity. Just remember that your past does not define you! Your actions do not define you. Your emotions do not define you. You are exactly who God says you are: His righteous, whole, complete-in-Him, precious child.

Your thoughts may go down paths you recognize are destructive, and you may need to practice controlling them. But as you immerse yourself in the Word of God, it will become much easier to begin to see things from God's perspective. You'll find that taking your thoughts captive becomes normal, until your mind is renewed and thinking positively becomes natural.

God loves you! He wants you to have an intimate relationship with Him so you can hear His voice clearly, think His thoughts, and see things from His perspective. No matter what has happened in your life to bring you to a place where you feel like all is lost, it isn't!

This is just the beginning.

> *Yet in all these things, You are more than a conqueror through Christ who loves you.*
>
> Romans 8:37

About the Author

CARLIE TERRADEZ is an international speaker, author, wife and mother of three amazing children. Born and raised in the United Kingdom, her family immigrated to the United States after she and her husband, Ashley, graduated from Bible college in 2008.

Shortly after her ordination, she became the co-founder of Terradez Ministries, a practical teaching ministry dedicated to empowering believers to walk in God's power and promises.

Carlie's life is a testimony to the miraculous power of God. She has been supernaturally healed from numerous life-threatening conditions, including epilepsy, and has also seen her terminally ill three-year-old daughter instantly recover. Carlie is passionate about helping others receive healing and walk in the abundant life that Jesus has provided for them.

HEART TO HEART
COUNSELING
CENTER

Heart to Heart Counseling Center located in Colorado Springs, Colorado specializes in sexual freedom counseling, treating intimacy anorexia, supporting spouse, as well as marital counseling and healing. For over thirty years, we have helped relationships heal after dealing with these issues, brought husbands and wives back together and helped couples find their intimacy again.

SERVICES
· 3 & 5 DAY INTENSIVES
· COUNSELING
· BOOKS
· DVDS

SPECIALITY
· SEXUAL FREEDOM
· PARTNERS OF ADDICTS
· PARENTS OF PRODIGALS
· INTIMACY ANOREXIA
· PARTNER BETRAYAL TRAUMA

ABOUT DR. DOUG WEISS

Dr. Douglas Weiss has been successfully counseling hurting hearts and relationships for more than 30 years. Dr. Weiss is a Licensed Psychologist and the Executive Director of Heart to Heart Counseling Center. He is an internationally known speaker and author. Dr. Weiss's own journey of recovery has equipped him with wisdom and compassion that goes well beyond his expert clinical skills.

The Harrison House Vision

Proclaiming the truth and the power

of the Gospel of Jesus Christ with excellence.

Challenging Christians

to live victoriously,

grow spiritually,

know God intimately.

Fast. Easy.
Convenient.

For the latest Harrison House product information and author news, look no further than your computer. All the details on our powerful, life-changing products are just a click away. New releases, email subscriptions, testimonies, monthly specials—find them all in one place. Visit harrisonhouse.com today!

harrisonhouse.com

Connect with us on

![f] Facebook @ **HarrisonHousePublishers**

and ![instagram] Instagram @ **HarrisonHousePublishing**

so you can stay up to date with news

about our books and our authors.

Visit us at **www.harrisonhouse.com**

for a complete product listing as well as

monthly specials for wholesale distribution.

.

MY JOURNEY TO THE ALTAR

MY JOURNEY TO THE ALTAR

Joyce Simpson

TATE PUBLISHING
AND ENTERPRISES, LLC

Published by Tate Publishing & Enterprises, LLC
127 E. Trade Center Terrace | Mustang, Oklahoma 73064 USA
1.888.361.9473 | www.tatepublishing.com

Tate Publishing is committed to excellence in the publishing industry. The company reflects the philosophy established by the founders, based on Psalm 68:11,
"The Lord gave the word and great was the company of those who published it."

Book design copyright © 2012 by Tate Publishing, LLC. All rights reserved.
Cover design by Nathan Harmony
Interior design by Jomel Pepito

Published in the United States of America

ISBN: 978-1-62147-211-7
1. Biography & Autobiography / Personal Memoirs
2. Biography & Autobiography / Religious
12.11.02

Acknowledgements

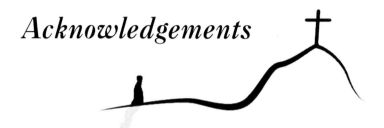

e mindful to always give thanks to God, for without His unwavering love and favor, this life would not be possible. "Give thanks to the Lord; call on His name; make known among nations what He has done" (1 Chronicles 16:8).

To my husband: "Two are better than one" (Ecclesiastes 4:9-12). "He who finds a wife finds a good thing, and obtains favor from the Lord" (Proverbs 18:22). "My power works best in your weakness" (2 Corinthians 12:8).

To my children: "You are my heart desired gifts from God. Every good and perfect gift is from above and comes down from the Father of lights" (James 1:17).

To my dear friends Kay, Emma, and Debbie: "Be devoted to one another in brotherly love. Honor one another beyond yourself" (Romans 12:10).

To my father: "Train up a child in the way he should go, and when he is old he will not depart from it" (Proverbs 22:6). Thank you for your love.

To my church and pastor: Thank you for teaching God's Word and God's embrace through your never-ending support groups, classes, testimonies, and many other tools used to win souls and strengthen our walk with Christ.

Table of Contents

Introduction

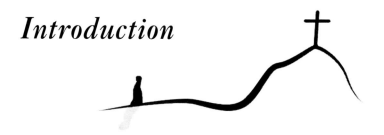

*A*s I reflect over the years of my life, I have used the avenues of marriage, children, family, and church to find happiness. After many years of ups and downs, joys and pains, disappointment after disappointment, the ultimate prize just never seemed to materialize. Sadly, I had no idea what the ultimate prize really was.

Since I was very young girl, I remember having an overwhelming desire to be a part of a successful, well functioning family. I grew up watching "Leave It to Beaver" and "Father Knows Best," and in my young adulthood, "The Cosby Show." Coming from a Southern background, God and family were deeply planted in my psyche. I knew as a young girl that I needed to get married and have children in order to be happy and successful. Strong morals and family were my desires for having a wonderful life and ultimate happiness.

Using this age-old formula for my life, I thought success was guaranteed. I also felt that by being determined, working hard, being honest, maintaining my integrity, and following the golden rule—"Do unto others as you would have them do unto you"—the American dream of marriage, children, career, happiness, and success was sure to be mine.

Not! I had my life all planned, but somewhere along the way, my spiritual knowledge was forgotten. I neglected God's plan and will for my life, and refused in my selfish state to put God's will first and wait on Him to bless me with the desires of my heart. When we strike out on our own, using our own abilities and understanding, we fail to ask for God's guidance and divine will in our lives. It is so easy for us to become sidetracked by the world's opinion of success.

On my journey, I lost focus in the many attempts to make my mark in the world. I assumed that as long as I loved the Lord and was a good person to others, He would keep me on the road to victory. I overcame trials and tribulations, remained headstrong, and believed that good would always triumph over evil. I was willing to adhere to God's plan as long as it was convenient and didn't interfere with my plans. Fooling myself, I continued on this path, believing that my minimal amount of living and believing in God's plan would somehow make me eligible for the prize.

Desires of the Heart

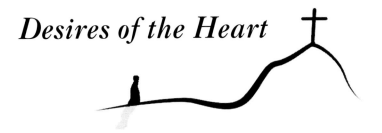

For as long as I can remember, I have always had a strong God-given desire to be part of a loving family. My parents were from the Deep South and were married at a very young age. My mother was just fifteen years old and my father five years her senior. Their marriage was arranged by their parents. I remember bursting with pride and relishing the story my dad would jokingly tell of my parents' wedding night. Because they were both virgins, they didn't know if the other was a man or woman and were not quite sure of what to do because of their naïveté and inexperience. What a pair of shoes to fill and a legacy on which to build a family. However, society would tell my generation a different story.

My mother was a stay-at-home mom and helper to her husband. My dad worked very hard on the family's farm and hired himself out to work on other people's farms. They lived with my father's family, together with some of his siblings and their children. My mother quickly became pregnant, and I was born after only fourteen months of marriage. Because my dad wanted a better life for his family, he decided to move from Alabama to the North when I was about a year old. Three years later, my sister was born, and our family began to grow.

After moving to the North, my dad became overwhelmed with cultural differences and lack of respect for the moral fiber in which his parents had raised him. But my mother delighted in the freedom from her upbringing. My dad felt displaced and uncomfortable in the crazy life of the city. He would have been happier back in the South surrounded by family. But my mother loved the excitement of the city with its many activities and her new-found freedom away from family constraints. This was a time when it was fashionable to be divorced. So my parents were divorced after having three children in less than ten years of marriage.

The divorce of my parents was one of the most devastating experiences of my life. Having lived a rather sheltered life, it was more horrible than I could have imagined. Dealing with the hurt of Daddy not coming home and me not being able to run and embrace him on a daily basis was just not conceivable in my small world. I was only nine years old.

This life-changing event started my quest and heartfelt desires to create the ultimate family life. I remember making up the ideal family when discussing family matters with classmates. "Yes, my parents are divorced, but my dad comes over often, calls all the time, and takes us places non-stop." (Yeah, I also had swamp land for sale). The truth of the matter was, my mother made it extremely difficult for my dad to come around. She was very bitter toward him despite the fact that she sought the divorce for her personal gain and satisfaction. I longed for the love and attention my father had lavished us with when we were still a family.

These longings became foremost in my thoughts. I imagined getting married at a young age, right out of high school, to my childhood sweetheart. These dreams occurred when I was only twelve years of age, but I was so determined to have this life. Unlike my parents, I would not fail. There was too much riding on my success, so I would manage to do what my parents had failed to do. This would be the ultimate prize! I was determined to have what I wanted—find the perfect boyfriend, fall in love, have fun, get married, and live happily ever after. This probably sounds like Cinderella, but like most girls, I love fairy tales.

Dating was difficult for me during my teen years. I went to live with my father and his new wife, and my dad held firm to a strong moral system and practices. In his mind dating was not acceptable until you finished high school. How could I find my husband if I couldn't date?

My father's mindset didn't stop my girlish dreams. I became passionate for many charitable causes and imagined myself righting the wrongs in life. Finally, I was allowed to date under very guarded circumstances. Although this was the middle of the 70s, the time when people's attitudes about sex and relationships were beginning to change, I was expected to practice the strong, moral teachings handed down from my southern grandparents. I was very naïve when it came to the games boys played, and the lies they told to achieve their goals. In high school I was not popular because I was just too serious for the average teen. God blessed me with the great body most girls dreamed of, but my attitude resembled a middle-aged woman who had too many worthwhile causes to die for. Yeah, that wasn't a turn-on to the young men! Consequently, I was not sought after—average looks, hot body but a middle-aged mindset. In plain English: for a teen, I was weird!

I managed to finish high school without being taken very seriously or making many friends. My father considered my ability to fight off the young men aiming for the ultimate prize, a major accomplishment. At this point in my life, I knew that to achieve my goals of having the family of my dreams, I needed to start making some serious moves in that direction. I was driven more to have a family than to experience life as a college student. Although education was very important to me, and I loved higher learning, I also had a great passion to complete my family life. It was a life that was interrupted in my childhood, and I just never had a sense of belonging after that. I had the old southern mindset to marry young, and I never considered being young and carefree like most my age. I didn't cherish young, wild, and free attitudes but was very old fashioned and mature beyond my years. So I devised the best plan. *What better place to find a man than church!* Why not start where I wanted to end up?

There was a family that I was familiar with, and their son had always been eager to engage in conversation with me. All the years we were in grade school together, he was considered the crème de la crème of all the boys in school. His family was in the ministry, and all the teachers treated him with favor. I shied away from him because he was too arrogant due to his family's position in the area. With some hesitation, I agreed to date him after he so diligently pursued me for months. My dad was always against a friendship with him, but I thought my father was just being rude and pushy. As the years go by, I can appreciate the wisdom of a father noticing the transparency of young men seeking their daughters out. I had the notion that if this young man was so eagerly interested in me, this must be a sign. My limited relationship with God was such that I was not cognizant of what an injustice I was unleashing upon myself. I jumped in with all I had, hoping this was the road to happiness. I befriended his sister and was polite and charming with his other family members and soon thought of them as the family I didn't have. This was my future we were talking about, and I couldn't leave anything to chance. I had to give it all I had. This would be the family I was deprived of in my childhood. This void was overtaking everything else in my life. I lived in an isolated state because my experiences with people in other families were limited. After my parents' divorce, I lived with my dad and stepmother and they had two children. I didn't really fit in and was never given the opportunity to accompany them on vacation. I was always excluded and never knew why except I was collateral damage from the first marriage and not a suitable fit in the second marriage. So with this young man, I never stopped to consider God in my planning process. The deep hurt that I never allowed God to be a part of was the same hurt that drove me to seek a personal solution. Had I sought out God's face, a life of service, and His divine guidance, my journey would have been blessed.

Moving forward in the story, this man was a conqueror. He took pride in obtaining the most unobtainable, least corrupt young ladies and adding them to his collection of trophies. I still held true to my old-fashion ways and upbringing. *No* was a constant word in my vocabulary. This young man was not equipped to respect a turn-down. For over a year, I managed to only be with him in the company of his sister or minister grandfather. On one occasion he convinced me that we needed a private moment so he could talk to me about his future with me. I was so hoping he would propose. But I was cornered, over powered, and alone. It was beyond humiliating, and it would take my entire young adult life to get over this gross violation to my body and mind and bring to me to a place of healing and restoration.

In the 70s, date rape was just beginning to surface. The use of the word *no* by women was still being debated. I was raped and then shock and fear consumed me when I found that I was pregnant. Not only had my body been violated, but my emotions were raw and totally destroyed. And now there was a child on the way. I simply shut down emotionally and remained silent, suffering the most hurtful shame and pain anyone can imagine. This was not supposed to happen to me. I was going for the fairy tale. After my child was born, I made all attempts to educate myself. Attending college with a baby out of wedlock was humbling in the midst of other single young girls. Judgment was all around me and I remained silent in my self-imposed prison. In my brokenness, I felt I let God down, and unforgiveness was the sentence I gave myself. My life was ruined and not worthy of God's love. My only hope was to raise my child, be the best mother I could, live my life out quietly, and not bring any attention to myself or my situation. I couldn't live down the shame and stigma I felt came with unwed mothers. I know the enemy comes to kill, steal, and destroy, but I allowed my own lack of knowledge of God's mercy to rob me of my self-worth. My family placed conditions on their love and support, and I had not met those conditions. Those conditions affected my acceptance of salvation, joy, and peace with God. I never looked to God—the true reflection of who we are—and His unconditional love. Now my self-worth was zero. I became my own worst enemy by not being able to forgive myself and turn to God for love and hope. I had no friends because I isolated myself from others out of fear of rejection and judgment. God's grace and mercy were not in my realm of awareness. I didn't realize how His love covers multitudes of sins, and that His grace is sufficient and will sustain us through anything.

After a while, I allowed myself to feel some hope and began to pray and think positively. I began to branch out, make friends, and even contemplated dating. I was optimistic in the flesh, full of worldly thinking, but still had not engaged in a solid relationship with God. I was yet to see myself as anything but a woman with a baby. My mindset was one that would have to settle for what I could get, since the fairy tale was now only a fairy tale. I know that *beggars can't be choosers*, so if a man wasn't a criminal and he didn't have a scandalous past—he could be a keeper. My family supported my self-loathing and they saw me as a failure and disappointment. Their words and deeds helped fuel my negative attitude of myself.

I took inventory of my assets, and of course my body was at the top of the list because I never considered my body as a temple and a living sacrifice. I viewed it as a means to get what I wanted or gain access to comfort. After all, I had already been horribly violated; the worst had already come to pass. My moral convictions had little or no meaning at this point. The enemy's lies defined who I was and what I could have. I overlooked God's ability to meet all my needs all the time. He can be a father, mother, brother, sister, and friend, but I was serving myself rather than serving Him. My focus changed and I was on a new path. I was determined to get all I could out of whatever circumstance I was in—self-gratification. When we don't make room for God, that space will be filled with something, and the enemy will manipulate our thought processes. I had gone from the fear of not being good enough to "I'm going to use what I have to get what I want." There was very little realization that my form of thinking was typical of women that have been sexually violated. Our society was on the brink of discovering how to assist women who were sexually assaulted, but the subject was still in the taboo stage. As uncomfortable as it was for law enforcement and the experts, it was twice as difficult for the victims. I learned to comfort and heal myself. I didn't know that God was protecting me from myself.

By the late 70s and early 80s, there seemed to be a sexual revolution, and morality was taking a backseat to sinful thought and deed. Folks were coming out of the closets on many levels. I was about to enter into spiritual warfare on the deepest level, fighting against principalities. I was becoming the classic example of "an idle mind is the devil's workshop." Because I didn't fill my life and mind with

Christ, I was an empty, young, abandoned vessel ripe for the filling.

After many years of meaningless relationships and uncertainty, I reevaluated my situation and revised my course of action. The enemy is relentless in his pursuit of us. If only we were so relentless in our pursuit of God. When I was totally engaged in wrong and sinful deeds, the notion I was wrong never entered my mind. I just encouraged myself to work harder. Although I still felt my opportunities were limited, somehow I had this false sense of security. God's grace was upon me even in my dark state of mind. I had wonderful neighbors, who knew me for my neighborhood mission projects—cooking, feeding the poor, and helping others. God still worked in my hard heart to be charitable to others.

I gained favor on my jobs; I always worked hard and helped others. I can see now that was a blessing from God over my life. God blessed me with the mind to work hard and to help others in spite of my own circumstances. God's grace and mercy shined through all the ugliness of my life. During some of my charitable works, I was introduced to a young man who had just graduated with a degree in social services. He was nice, came from a two-parent family, and attended church sometimes. He seemed to be taken with me and my daughter, and I thought, "*He's not what I want, but he will do. It's a man that wants to marry me, a lady with a baby.*" I thought, "*How foolish I would be to pass this up. It would give me a sense of belonging and respect. I could hold my head up and shine as the mother and wife I longed to be.*" Because I didn't feel worthy of even this much, I'd better jump on this. I'm fairly easy to get along with, and I can be very accommodating, especially with my self-esteem at an all-time low. The agony I inflicted on myself was unbelievable. I didn't have the wherewithal to avoid being taken in by society's stigmas. All along I convinced myself that the marriage was great and would launch me into the "honorable woman" status. We allow society to place such pressure on social standings that we are driven to have a chunk of the dream. The dream, to me, was having a husband, two or more children, two cars, two-car garage home, lakefront vacation property, money in the bank, and lots of friends with the same.

Now coming from a strict, southern, religious, background, these desires were not far off the path. I thought marriage would allow me to lift my head up with pride and accomplish greatness in ways not possible before, due to all my fears and judgment. I campaigned long and hard for my new role in a made-to-order marriage. I loved cooking, cleaning, and being the modern day "June Cleaver" housewife diva. I worked outside the home, but I still enjoyed cooking for my family and seeing my husband eat. Boldness emerged. I began to be comfortable in my skin, and feelings of inadequacy were gone. A new woman arrived on the scene, and it was me. I was confident, vivacious, and just plain arrogant in many ways I'd never been before. I developed a sense of style that had only lurked in the shadows before. I was transformed into a woman who was not afraid to try and do all the things she dreamed of doing. I showered my husband with affection in appreciation of my newfound freedom.

About a year into the marriage, my husband began to make demands for a child of his own even though he loved the daughter I had brought into the marriage. I was very turned off by the demand for another child. I was enjoying my new life, and I wanted more children, just not at that moment. It was still about me. I took a real hard look at him and his family and wasn't sure about more children at this point. His family was not a fan of me; they wanted more for their son than to be saddled with a lady and her child. I was determined to prove them wrong. I would be an asset to their son's life, and they would not see me in that manner for long.

I worked hard to contribute to the family budget; actually I contributed more than my husband did. I wanted to overcome the stigma of having a child out of wedlock and get beyond the judgment I felt from his family. But he still wanted his own child, so I agreed to get pregnant. After about six months of trying, we conceived a son.

After our son was born, life was delightful. It was a wonderful experience giving birth with a husband beside you. I enjoy caring for children and giving them attention on demand. It created so much energy in my life. My son was very demanding, due to some illnesses, and was partial to my attention. This made his father somewhat jealous, and he bonded even more with my daughter. Because of my son's needs, I found it very difficult to work outside the home, so eventually I became a stay-at-home mom. Being a stay-at-home mom is very rewarding yet disappointing if you expect appreciation for anything more in life than being a domestic.

I didn't like asking my husband for money, and felt like I was placing my burdens on him. I still harbored some feelings of shame about having a child prior to marriage, and I did not want my husband to feel weighed down by my issues. While at home I discovered that I really loved working with small children. It was a gift from God. I determined to make a career of this much-needed profession. For the first time in my life, it seemed that I could have something I wanted that was just for me. This was a chance to right so many wrongs and injustices by creating a business and tailoring rules that suited my lies and desires. Here again, selfishness breeds sin, and doing good deeds with the wrong motives has consequences. Unknowingly, my life would take a new direction.

Reflections

As I read back over this chapter that I wrote many years ago, I realize even in my writings I still hesitated to embrace God's love for me. I remained bonded to shame and unforgiveness. I placed the entire burden upon myself. The Word teaches us that we have needless burdens and shame when we don't take everything to God in prayer. My burden and shame stemmed from not being able to tell the truth and the complete story of what happened to me. I felt that somehow I should have been able to prevent the outcome. I wanted the young man who violated me to realize what he had done and even decide to marry me to atone for his sin. But I believed that speaking out against him would provoke anger and ruin my chances of legitimacy.

The truth is, it wasn't wrong for me to desire these things. They were desires placed in my heart by God. I often fail to let God carry out His plans for my life. I allowed myself to be worn down by my insecurities and by people I perceived to be more worthy than myself.

This young man was the grandson of a prominent minister in the area. His family gained the respect of teachers in the community. But they displayed a great sense of divine privilege and allowed their offspring to wreak havoc on others. They used the community and church as their personal amusement park and took advantage of the honor given them for being leaders and shepherds of God's Word.

When betrayal happens from an unlikely source where reputation should be protected and honorable, one has a feeling beyond explanation. My level of trust was damaged; my sense of direction was distorted. When the very people who teach the gospel betray the Word and live a lie, the shattering realization left me not knowing what to do. My survival mode was activated. I retreated to the comforts of the only person I felt I could trust—myself, until God restored my faith. I never lost faith in Whom God is. I lost faith in who I was to God. I wrestled with my worthiness and my guilt over not working harder to keep myself pure. I struggled for years with so much unforgiveness, and this kept God from healing me and restoring me sooner. I emerged into a world of self and vowed to remain quiet and away from the general population, especially the so-called Christians.

I know that it was foolish to bear a shame that was not mine and entertain the thoughts of this man ever being anything than what he was—a rapist of pride, dignity and God's gift of virginity.

Our society has come a long way since 1977. God has allowed us as people to recognize a woman's right to say *No* without consequences. Date rape has been exposed for what it is, and there are laws and recourse for young women that weren't in place during my season.

1. Have you ever set out to do things on your own only to realize that your desires are God's will for your life?
2. When this happened, what was the end result and why?
3. Were you able to evaluate the purpose of the results?
4. At what point did you seek God's wisdom and sovereignty?
5. How did you allow the Lord to redirect your path for a favorable outcome?

In my case I was so beaten down spiritually that I couldn't see myself as God saw me. I placed value on my life according to the world's standards. Having my eye on the vision of the world kept me from seeing God's grace, mercy, and beauty. My lack of knowledge of God's Word prevented me from processing who I was in Christ Jesus. My focus was based on a narrow view of myself according to my circumstances. Until I could see past my situation and receive the spirit of God in my life I would continue to wrestle with my self-image.

Detour

B eing a person of great ambition, I wanted to start my own business, so after careful research and consideration, I decided to own and operate a preschool center. This allowed me the opportunity to spend time with my baby and do the things I loved such as cooking, cleaning, and making children laugh and feel safe.

Children always made me feel very capable and loved. It was an opportunity to serve and care for little people who are nonjudgmental and make you feel worthy in your purpose. *How wonderful*, I thought, *to be able to go to work, dress casually, and play all day.* What a great job! Thanks to God, I found the perfect location for my business. It was a frame house with lots of large, custom windows. On snowy or rainy days, the children could look out and see small animals scurrying about the yard. There was over an acre of yard space and it was surrounded by Fortune 100 companies and upper-middle class real estate.

Trying to start a business as a woman was a bit difficult at first. Many doors were closed in my face, but I soon learned how to reopen those doors. After the first six months of business, there was hardly an opening for a child. The waiting list was at least a year, sometimes longer depending on the age of the child. This was a blessing I took credit for. At this point, I was full of myself. I thought all of this was happening because of my wonderful talents and skills. I never gave God my praise or glory. I began to excel and exceed my own expectations. Note that I said *"I."* The huge mistake I made was leaving God, who opened doors to make this all possible. Lesson learned later: Never take on any project and leave the Lord out if you truly want to be successful.

With every growing moment of my success, my husband was becoming more bitter and jealous. He believed his education and experience were superior to mine. He told me that if anyone deserved this kind of success, it was him! And, he told me this every chance that he got. I ignored his comments and negative attitude and told myself that this would pass. I was so wrapped up in myself, though, and I ignored him and all the signs of verbal abuse. The thrill of being in control of my destiny was the most wonderful experience I had ever felt. I didn't consider that my Savior had anything to do with this, because I believed my accomplishments were of my own merit. Not one time did I consider that the gifts that I had came from above. Looking back, I compare myself to a teen just graduating from high school. Often they think they are adults and don't need their parents anymore. They are cocky and full of themselves. As parents, we allow our children the opportunity to grow up, and often they fall on their faces. I imagine the Lord allows us, His children, to do the same. Like many teenagers, we later realize that we need the help and wisdom of someone more knowledgeable than ourselves. Some of us have to fall several times. We hit our heads on a sharp rock only to get up again and try it several more times. Oh, what a wonderful, forgiving God we serve! He shows us favor and mercy when we fall short of His will. Sure, I had been taught, knew, and had had a good understanding of where my blessing came from. It seems like it would have been easy for me to be in the spirit of praising the Lord for all that had taken place. Well, some of us are slow learners.

I was having the best time of my life and taking full advantage of it. I deemed that I deserved this life after all the hardships that I had experienced over the years. Mind you, at this point I was only twenty-four years old. I really should have been on my knees, thankful that I even had a mind mature enough to start a business. Business was great. The clients were pleased with the educational program and even recommended our school to friends, family, and coworkers. I had a difficult time finding good employees, but that was a small issue to deal with compared to the huge benefits I was reaping from being an entrepreneur.

The more successful I was, the more verbally abusive my husband became. This began to affect my ability to relate to others. I lashed out verbally to my staff and any adults who opposed me. I learned to use my mouth as a weapon of mass destruction, and the only limit to my rage was that I always managed to keep it from the children. I saw children as my only allies. Everyone else who was in range, was blasted. My words were a defense mechanism against the wrongs that were done to me. Lashing out was my way of fighting feelings of insecurity that had overwhelmed me so many times in the past. God teaches us that a still tongue carries a wise head. According to that proverb, I wasn't the brightest bulb on the Christmas tree.

I was self-serving. I had never felt appreciated for my achievements or intelligence, and didn't understand that I shouldn't have looked to man to reward or acknowledge my gifts and talents. My talents were gifts from above and should have been used to the glory of God, His will, and His purpose.

My children were getting older, which allowed me to have a more flexible schedule. I shopped, went to happy hour, and traveled with girlfriends, mostly unmarried girlfriends. Being with unmarried friends led to issues because of different priorities. I stayed away from home to avoid any verbal confrontations. I was a successful business owner and was not about to let anyone put me down. As long as I kept this frame of mind, I felt the abuse was not affecting me. How wrong I was!

When we are in a self-serving mode, we often make excuses for the things we do. I had to party with my friends because I worked hard, had a lot of responsibilities, and needed an outlet to release stress. I stayed healthy and happy by going out to eat, drinking, and spending time with anyone other than my spouse. Remember the reason I married him in the first place? Now I had greater self-esteem because I was making a contribution to society and being acknowledged. Many parents have deep feelings of appreciation and love toward those who care for their children. My profession was so rewarding, and my ego was really being stroked.

Years passed and my bank account was growing along with my confidence. I was still under the gun at home, but it didn't matter because I was on top in my profession. Who cared what my husband thought anyway? My relationship with my children was great. I spent wonderful time with them. My friends, family, and employees seemed to overlook my Dr. Jekyll and Mrs. Hyde routine.

I began to believe that I was too good for this common man who was my husband. The enemy can deceive us by making us believe that we are better than another person. I was about to make a very costly discovery and mistake. We were friendly toward each other for the sake of our children and appearance. It was easy to be his friend. He was a social person with a good sense of humor when he wasn't verbally lashing out at me. We developed a brother and sister type relationship early in our marriage. This manner of relationship was just going nowhere. It had no fulfillment and no foundational structure. After awhile I asked for a divorce. In many cultures and religious denominations divorce is common and acceptable—nothing lasts for ever. My husband was opposed to the idea, throwing a fit each time that I asked. I never planned to behave badly, but the situations I was in were conducive to bad behavior. I failed to surround myself with practicing Christian married couples with strong morals.

I only prayed as a routine method of keeping the door open just in case I needed God in the future. What a lame way of thinking and dishonoring God, Creator of everything. My prayers were generic. These prayers were insulting, to say the least, to Almighty God, but I thought they were sincere. I didn't seek to have a relationship with God because I didn't want to be convicted about the lifestyle or the choices I was making. After all, we do have a sense of right and wrong given to us by God along with freedom of will.

I kept high standards. After all, my family lineage was the example. I began to think that I could do better without this man and that he was just not the man for me. As I look back I see how unequally yoked we were. Our families were so different. Our values and views of family were different. His family's religion offered more freedom when it came to sexuality and acceptance of practices the Bible clearly states are wrong. I believed that my husband was just not the man for me and certainly could not be the man God wanted me to have. I used things that I knew about him to justify my exit from the marriage. Remember I picked this man and didn't seek God in the matter. I was determined to change my situation at almost any cost, not realizing that the cost might be more than I was willing or could afford to pay.

I allowed myself to communicate with other men on a friendly basis. I knew it was not appropriate for a married woman, but told myself that I was only talking to them. It was nice to see that I was attractive to other men, men who in the past would not have given me the time of day. At least those were my thoughts based on feelings of poor self-worth. My newfound confidence was still hiding insecurities and imperfections from the general public.

The enemy can deceive us and have us taking pleasures in relationships that are on the human level trying to fill what we lack on a spiritual level. My desires for the fairytale romance with a knight in shining armor to whisk me away to a house on the beach to live happily ever after, were void without God. The grass always appears greener on the other side, until you hop over the fence only to realize there are weeds and erosion unless you apply appropriate fertilizer.

This has been a trick of the enemy since the beginning of time and the fall of man in the Garden of Eden. We are attracted to the things that will bring us fame, fortune, and romance. While these things are not forbidden, they are gifts that only God can give; they are not ours for the taking. All things must work within God's order and plan for our lives, otherwise we just promote our freewill over God's will.

Like so many others before me, I felt I knew what was best for my life. I would make empty promises to the Lord. At times I found myself begging and making bargains with the Lord. I'm sure none of you have ever done that. But if I'm the only one, I can tell you that God doesn't respond to our "if-only" prayers. I would foolishly pray and ask the Lord, *If only you bless me with a husband that I want, I will go to church more.* I had a ton of these preposterous prayers. I was falling short in so many areas of my life. I particularly had an issue with tithes. I added up my newfound fortune and decided that 10 percent was just too much money to give the church. I reasoned in my mind that this church was not worthy of my contribution because of their tolerance for sexual immorality. Now, I had become an expert on interpreting the Holy Word of God to suit my personal whims. Boy, was I headed for a major melt down. I wasn't ashamed to cheat God out of what was His. I was unaffected by the fact that I was living comfortably and giving God the leftovers.

As I'm writing this, I'm thinking, *Do I really want my readers to know how broken and fallen I was?* I have no choice. The only way God can get the glory is for you to know my brokenness. The Lord's goodness exceeds anything I could ever imagine; He will transform us in spite of our total disregard for Him. When we repent and turn from our evil ways, He restores and blesses us in ways we never imagine. When it's all said and done, we get to spend eternity with Him and enjoy the splendor of His love.

Okay, let's tally my life up so far. I was talking to other men, ignoring my blessings, not giving 10 percent of my earnings in honor of God. I was selfishly motivated. I was clueless. I can't say I would have been smart enough not to stand under a tree in a thunderstorm at this point. My mindset is puzzling to me. Being blinded by sin has that effect. My life was a hot mess!

I knew that I needed to improve my relationship with the Lord, but I avoided Christians. I was still blaming my hardships in life on those claiming to be Christians who had hurt me. Telling the Lord I wasn't leaving Him, I left the church. I analyzed my situation foolishly. I was a good person, a law-abiding citizen, a good mother, wife, and provider, and I grew up in the church. I could afford to indulge myself awhile. After all, I deserved it. I was young and had my entire life to become a proper Christian. I was already behaving better than most. I grew up with a self-righteous mother, and the Bible warns us about self-righteousness. I deserved death, but God thought otherwise and sent His only son Jesus.

I want to write kinds of things in this book that most people are afraid to admit. We can be somewhat effective hiding from the criticism of others, but we can never escape the judgment of God. I failed to assemble myself with other believers who could challenge my thinking and behavior. Without challenge, we often have the tendency to think that our thoughts are correct. There is strength in numbers, and we should surround ourselves with other Christ believers and doers of the Word. Being a Christian fallen from grace is a difficult state of mind. I was not living a life according to the Word of God and was unaware of the impact it had on my life.

Each of us needs to make sure we keep a prayer warrior in our lives. You need a Christian friend with whom you can share your fears, secrets, shortcomings—every aspect of your life. You need a friend that you can grow with in Christ and be committed to helping each other stay focused—someone who will tell you the hard truth and remind you of the gospel. I had such a dear friend, Emma. She was a sweet, older lady, but I insulated myself from her. I even made her life difficult while she was working for me.

I had another close friend, Kay. We were both young and unwise in the ways of the Lord, and we both had marital problems at the same time. It was difficult to let her into my world because I viewed her as being so beautiful, educated, and successful, and I didn't want her to know my life was a mess. She always seemed to have it all—a supportive mother and great sisterly love. I fell short in this area and was afraid to be transparent out of fear of rejection for not measuring up. She knew me better than anyone and still had only scratched the mere surface. I would only tell her about 85 percent, and the other percent I just didn't tell or made up something to fill in the pieces of my life. I never wanted anyone to know the horrible things that had been done to me in life. I never wanted to admit my mother's utter contempt for me. I wanted to measure up to the ideal family. My friend was everything I dreamed of being. I now know she was placed in my life for sisterly love by God. Even when I was distant from the Lord, He provided me with a support system that would later prove to be a God-sent blessing. Our Lord is magnificent! In darkness when we are removed from fellow believers, He never leaves or forsakes us. He makes provisions for our future needs and makes a path of repentance, redemption, and a coming-home feast. The Lord prepared me to come crawling back, humbled by His grace and my life failures. When we live life with the world, doing worldly things, we share that life with friends. The same is true for a life with God; we share it with friends. God wants us to lift Him up so souls can be saved by the godly lives we live.

My girlfriend, Kay, and I were at similar stages in our lives, but she lived three hundred miles away. We both were in marriages that had proven not to be suitable in our limited visions, but we didn't fully understand all of the events taking place. Both of us were from families of divorce and both were dealing with verbally abusive husbands. We have been blessed over our years of friendship to talk regularly on the phone. We focused on our friendship and trusted that no matter what life dished out, we would handle it together. We loved each other and didn't know that our love and friendship would be challenged but would survive immeasurable events. Since we were prayer partners, we struggled and pressed on to have a life in Christ. The Lord knew we would rely on one another's spiritual gifts to find our way back to life with God. God gives each of us different talents and spiritual gifts to compliment His love for us and to serve as a help to each other.

I was still focused on me, and all I could achieve. I have always been the type of person who didn't want to be in the spotlight and took this to the extreme in most cases due to insecurities. Now, I had become bolder, willing to take on the world, armed with a few deceptions of the enemy (pride and self-righteousness). I combined my passion for loving and taking care of children with my selfish desires. Had I truly been serving the Lord, I would have been fulfilled with my service unto children. I relied on my abilities, which were unraveling before my eyes. I had blinders on, and the enemy had set me up for temporary success then failure and destruction.

I lost my wherewithal to know that there was success and power in the name Jesus, who was waiting in the wings for me to call on Him. All I had to do was repent and turn from my ways, humble myself before Him and become His faithful servant before God.

The Lord wants us to be faithful unto Him, not worship our abilities or place money or success above Him. I never realized that this is what I was doing. I would have never offended the Lord on purpose, but yet I was ignoring His Word. I was in direct disobedience because I wasn't reading His Word or putting Christian behavior into practice. The kingdom is too wonderful to ignore, but I was blinded by all the distraction that is a part of worldly living.

Again, armed with my success, financial stability, new attitude, and, I might add, new sexy look (I got a makeover), I felt all things were possible. Still, I ignored that all good things come from God.

Reflections

At this point in my life, I was about twenty-six years of age with two children, and I really didn't know how to live a Christian life. The lives that had been modeled before me were my widowed maternal grandmother and paternal grandparents that all lived seven hundred miles away. The foundation for Christianity was present, but the representation wasn't readily available or accessible within my immediate circle of family and friends. Everyone was so self-absorbed in the early 80s. Life was about making things happen, achieving greater things than the generation before us, and having more exposure to the world around us. I was exploring and creating new boundaries and ripping down barriers and replacing them with nothing of substance. Our culture was creating new definitions and justifying our sins and the sins of others.

One of the more popular viewpoints was redefining and tailoring religion to suit our selfish desires. This allows wickedness to deceive our perception of God's laws. I was caught up in making life good for myself and my family and taking steps to right the wrongs in my life. But these things were only right in my eyes, not in God's eyes. My reasoning had no foundation in Christ. Instead it was grounded in worldly things based on my physical and financial ability to make choices.

I thrived in my God-given talents and blessings, but I lacked appreciation from whence they came. I lacked wisdom and just plain biblical wherewithal to withstand the trials of everyday life. I was unwise in all my ways. I was double-minded, prone to pride, and unaware of the adversary and his methods of deceit.

When we fail to acknowledge that the world is in the clutches of the devil, we play right into his hands. He wants us to go about our daily lives thinking of him as a harmless animated character with red horns and a tail. He preys upon us, and he has his way with us unless we submit our lives to God under the blood of Jesus. Only in Christ can we have victory over the snares of Satan. To know God is to love Him. The only way we can know Him is by reading and studying His Word; praying for wisdom; and putting into practice a lifestyle of service, biblical teaching, and dedication to living for and with God.

1. When things are going well for you, do you find yourself less in touch with God? Or more in touch?
2. Explain in detail what ways are helpful in maintaining a healthy relationship with God.
3. Can you remember times in your life where you didn't make time to include God in everyday applications?
4. Have you ever felt you were in control of your life and the choice you made would determine the outcome?
5. Now how do you view yourself being in control?
6. Are you a person that will seek help and ask for wise, godly advice from others, and then consider the advice and apply it?

God's Word is the best advice, and He covers every topic known to man in His Word, the Bible. What a wonderful God to consider beforehand all the wisdom and advice we would need and supply it in His written Word and teachings.

God's Word reminds me of buying a product and the owner's manual is included along with a written warranty guarantee. You can call customer service 24/7, and you can get replacement parts. We are God's "product"—made in His image. He is available 24/7 and He continues to shape us to become more and more suitable and pleasing to Him. Our sins are washed in the blood of the lamb, cleaned, saved, and set aside to be used for God's purpose and will. And even more than that, we get eternal life with God.

Flesh Versus Spirit

*T*he world continued to lay claim on the lives of my husband and me. He had become more self-centered and engrossed in acquiring material things—foreign cars, expensive suits and shoes, and he played golf several times a week. I had never been materialistic; I was always comfortable with simple things and looking plain. However, I did begin to make statements in other ways. My self-esteem had improved, and I flaunted it through my attitude. Entertaining was fun and because I was from the South, cooking and eating were a big part of life. Having parties and family gatherings were a few things we still shared. But the more my income increased, the more he spent, and the angrier I got. I resented the fact that he was spending much more than he was making; he was living high-on-the-hog on my income. I was more the conservative one. His family, who showed nothing but contempt for me, only used me for what I could give them. But I buried my feelings about all of this because I was finally feeling good about me. Consequently, I was determined not to let anyone upset my world and my newfound comfort zone. Now I know that being surrounded by my husband and his family of nonbelievers was exactly where the enemy wanted me to be. It was physically and mentally draining. I began to feel even unhappier with my husband and confided this to Kay and one of my sisters. Things continued going downhill, and I asked my husband for a divorce. He told me that because I worked over sixty hours a week, he would probably look more favorable in front of a judge in obtaining custody of the children. He counted on his threats and my love for my children to play upon my fears. This kept me quiet for a while longer. Beneath my quietness, however, I became resentful and determined that I would get even with him for his threats.

I began to stay out more, exclude my husband from my circle of friends, travel, and ignore him as a man and as a husband. I complained about him and became just as verbally abusive to him as he was to me. I told myself I would stay with him until the children graduated from high school and not a day longer. But until then, I would go where I pleased and see who I wanted. This was a behavior that was acceptable in my circle of friends. It was also a behavior indicative of the times we were living in during the late 80s and early 90s. As you can imagine, my actions caused a lot of strife. Arguments and tension were between us all the time, but I didn't care. It was "an eye for an eye" now. We made every attempt to shield our children and agreed on some warfare rules to keep the kids out of the line of fire. We never, and I mean never, argued or raised our voices in our home. We always conducted our battles via phone during work hours. When he was home, I was never at home. I usually got dinner for the family and then went back to my office after the kids were asleep. I came up with creative ways about when to be at home and not be there. I would never advocate behaving in this manner, but we did manage to keep the kids pretty unaware.

I refused to be a wife in the physical sense and of course this just fueled his fire. He was frustrated and angry most of the time. With the anger directed toward me, I was energized by the power and affect I was having on him. I was not interested in a physical relationship with him. His meager income was a turn-off to me, so it was easy to abstain from him. Whenever he approached me, I would say awful things to make him even angrier. Our marriage became a battle of the wills, and I was not going to be defeated. Now this is the kind of stuff Satan loves. He had me targeted, and I was holding the bull's-eye right at my head. How spiritually out of touch was I?

Well, continue on, my readers.

There were no holds barred in our verbal battles, and I tried to spend the money before he could, buying senseless things that were of no value to our family or us. I planned vacations and stayed in the most expensive hotels. I even invited his family along on trips. During this time God was still trying to get my attention. He would prick my conscience and cause me to feel guilty about my behavior. But I would quickly dismiss God's words and replace them with my husband's words. "Before I let you divorce me, I will take you to the cleaners. You will be begging on the streets. I will have all your money and the kids." I would think, *How dare you, when God gave all of this to me.* I used God's name when it was helpful to me. I tried to use God to justify why I had so much, but I never acknowledged that all I had was really God's. He was allowing me to be a steward over it, and I was not being a good steward.

By now, I had begun to gain more attention from men. This attention was addicting, and it helped me thrive in a hostile environment. I took full advantage of the attention and used it to stroke my ego and fuel my pride. I was angry and prideful, very ripe for a fall.

Some of my old insecurities began to resurface, and I felt as if I were doomed in a worthless relationship. I believed that this man was not good enough for me, and if I had to be married, I was not going to follow the rules of marriage. As for the children, I was going to make sure that they were sheltered from any problems between us. I really do thank

God now for shielding my children. Marital issues and divorce are devastating for children, and the Lord placed His arms around my children during this time. In spite of all the craziness, people still thought we were the model couple. We managed to maintain our images in public. Like I said earlier, it was easy to be friendly with my husband. He was in social service work so he understood the importance of keeping it together during ugly times. I now can give God alone credit for shielding the children and answering my prayers for them. How faithful God was to me even in my sinful state. I knew we weren't the happy couple, and the deceit was eating me up inside since I longed to have a loving husband. How long could I continue to live a lie? I was bursting at the seams and only shared this with a few people due to fear of being judged. If I revealed the problems, the truth of why I married this man would have to come out. It all would fall on me; I would have to be transparent before man.

I remained a hardworking woman, working more than seventy hours a week by then. I couldn't count on my marriage, but I could count on my business. I made it a priority and gave it and the children my primary focus.

I was at work about 12:30 p.m. the Thursday before Memorial Day in 1991 when I received a phone call. The female voice on the other end frantically asked, "Do you have a ten-year-old daughter?"

I asked, "Who is this? I have a twelve-year-old daughter."

The voice went on to say, "I am a nurse from St. Anthony's Hospital Emergency Room, about seventy minutes from St. Louis where you live. We have your daughter and sister. They have been in an automobile accident, and your daughter is brain dead. Your sister is stabilized but unresponsive."

I was standing at my desk holding the phone. The next thing I knew I was on my knees calling out the only name I knew to call. *"Dear Lord, no! Not my child, dear Lord!"* My staff rallied around me and tried to pry the phone from my hands. Within a matter of seconds, the Lord gave me the strength and the mind to stand and get back on the phone. I asked the nurse, "What level trauma center are you?"

She replied, "We are not equipped to deal with traumas of this magnitude."

I pleaded, "Please tell me the hospital location and stay on hold while I call her doctor." I placed her on hold and I called the pediatrician at his office. Surprisingly, he answered the phone. How awesome God is! What doctor answers his/her own phone in an office with six other attending physicians, seven nurses, and two receptionists? I began to scream the situation to him. He asked where she was and then placed me on hold. Within minutes he came back to the phone. When a tragedy occurs, situations that are only minutes seem longer than they really are. The doctor's voice said, "Hang in there, the medical helicopter is leaving St. Louis right now to get your daughter and bring her back. You need to stay by the phone. The helicopter nurse may need vital information." Our pediatrician was in contact with the attending hospital and our children's hospital giving them information as they needed it.

The Lord continued to strengthen me to make calls. I called my parents and husband. I asked my husband to contact an ambulance and arrange to have my sister transported to St. Louis also. About an hour later, we got a call from the helicopter medic who told me things weren't good and my daughter would probably die in route. He told me that he would stay with her and hold her hand so she wouldn't be alone. I told him to tell her that I loved her and to think about Jesus. He asked me if I would like him to put the headset near her so she could hear me. I then told her if she could hear me, I loved her. I started saying the Lord's Prayer and Psalm 23.

As the helicopter approached our city, they called and said that my daughter was still alive and told us to come to the hospital. By this time, my husband had arrived from work to pick me up. My mother was with me, and my staff and a few clients surrounded us. We departed together and made our way to the hospital. As we turned into the hospital entrance, we could hear the helicopter landing on the roof. A chill went down my spine. When we arrived at the front desk, a host of the hospital staff was waiting for us. They whisked us to a private room. Prior to that, we got a glimpse of the paramedics rushing her down the hall. Had I not know that was my child, I would not have recognized her. She was swollen to four times her normal size. The hospital administrators tried to comfort us by keeping us posted on her condition. By then it was 4:00 p.m. I sat and prayed, unable to stop my leg from shaking because of nerves. I remember my husband becoming angry with me because I couldn't stop shaking my leg. Even in this situation, the bitter seeds that we had sown continued to grow. I ignored him. I was a mother in the front of a battle for my child's life. I needed all of my resources and I didn't consider him to be one of them. I allowed the enemy to poison my mind against him.

I made more necessary phone calls. I called Kay, who had just left her husband and was traveling miles to her hometown. I called upon my dear friend Emma, the older lady whom I had driven from working with me because of my sinful behavior. I hadn't talked to her in years. She was at a missionary meeting, and I left a message with her son. She immediately left the meeting, bringing all the missionaries with her. Emma was older, and to me she was a big sister and mother figure. She had five children and a strong, successful, Christian marriage. As the hours passed, more people found out what had happened. About 7:00 p.m., the doctors called us in for a briefing. We were informed that my daughter had a traumatic brain injury, TBI, and internal bleeding from her spleen. If they tried to repair or remove the spleen, it would be sudden death due to her condition, and she would not survive surgery. They also said that she had lost her left eye. Her condition was grave, and she wasn't expected to live twenty-four hours. I wanted to see her, but they said not yet. They asked us if we would consider organ donation, but I couldn't give up yet. They told me that if she lived; she would be a vegetable for the rest of her life.

We returned to the waiting room. I begged and pleaded with God and prayed the prayers that most of us would in a situation like this. I pleaded with God not to take my child. I would do anything He wanted; just don't take my child. I kept repeating my words as if the Lord had not heard me. I wanted to make sure that he knew how serious I was about this. I wanted Him to do what I wanted, even though I had done none of what He wanted. Now I was in no position to be calling the shots. I refused to pray the prayer "Let your will be done" because I did not want His will to be death. I was still hanging onto my selfish whims. I just wanted God to make her better.

About 8:00 p.m., a security officer from the lobby called to the waiting room for me. He said, "I've never seen anything like this before. There are about two hundred people in the lobby for you, and we can't allow them to come to the intensive care floor, so you have to come down." I went down, and saw Emma, missionaries from her church, a community of people from our neighborhood, business clients, and church members! Oh my Lord, how mighty is your love! We prayed, and I thanked them for coming, and then went back upstairs. On the verge of physical and mental exhaustion, I did the only thing I could do. I was in the perfect position for *total surrender*. I was broken. I was beat down. I had fallen into a bottomless pit of shame and sin. I stopped praying a prayer to save my child, and I prayed instead: "Lord, I come before you sinful and broken but thankful for being able to call upon your help! Forgive me, Lord, I have been selfish, undeserving of anything, especially your love, grace, and mercy. I am not going to ask you not to take my child when you gave your only Son to save my miserable self. I ask you to give me strength to get through this and to let your will be done. Walk with me, Lord, and save me from the life I have so selfishly made a mess of. Amen"

As soon as I finished my prayer, I walked toward the intensive care unit. My husband asked, "Where are you going? You know you can't get in to see her." I told him, "I need to see my child, say good-bye, and let her know she is going to see God." As I walked down the long corridor, the nurse met me. She stated, "I was just coming to get you. Your daughter is stable, and the bleeding has stopped." Medically, a bleeding spleen just doesn't stop bleeding on its own. Glory to God, the divine healer, who stopped the bleeding.

I walked into the intensive care unit, and there were so many very ill children. I went to my daughter's bed. Her long flowing hair had been shaved. She was hooked to nine machines. A bolt and cables came from her brain. I touched her. "Mommy is here, but I can't do anything to help you. If you can hear me, you need to think about Jesus. He loves you more than you know. Think about the Lord's Prayer and Psalms 23" (our children had attended Christian schools since pre-k so they knew Christ, though not by me modeling it). After saying *I love you*, I left her in God's mighty hands and returned to the waiting room.

The next morning, Friday, the doctors briefed us and still wanted us to consider organ donation. There was a little girl next to my daughter that needed a heart and lungs, and my daughter was a match. I told them that it was not up to me; it was up to God. I couldn't make that decision at that point. She had survived the night, which was good. The doctors assured me that she would never walk or talk again, and if she ever came out of the coma, she would be in a vegetative state. This had very little effect on me. I was under the protection of the Lord and had put on the full armor of God to withstand the wiles of the devil. I was not about to go backward. It was time for me to go back to my roots of early knowledge of Christ and plant myself to not be moved again. My life was not my own, and for so long I had behaved as if I was in control of this life.

The mother in me still feared the unknown, but I trusted God and was ready for the task ahead. After forty-eight hours, the doctors were still unchanging. They asked if they could remove life support. At this time it seemed to be best, so I went to say good-bye. Life support was removed, but my daughter began to breathe on her own, so I had them reattach life support. I had not left the hospital since Thursday, and it was now Sunday. My sister had suffered some difficulties due to the trauma of the news of my daughter, so I needed to go the hospital where she was, twenty minutes away, to be with her during and after her heart surgery. She was beyond consoling, for on their way out of town, she had fallen asleep behind the wheel of the car and caused the crash. I had been scheduled to travel with my sister out of town but had an inspection of my office, which resulted in my not being able to go with them. I stayed with my sister awhile assuring her all would be fine, and then I returned to my child. It was during this time that I felt the overwhelming presence and peace of the Lord. I stayed at my daughter's bedside and ran my business from the hospital. I showered, slept, and ate there. After all, the Lord spared her life. I felt that because I had been so awful over the past years, I didn't have the nerve to ask the Lord for more. My friend, Emma reminded me of God's grace and the need to rely on my knowledge of Christ to trust Him and accept His goodness.

For the next three months while my daughter lay in the hospital, fighting to come out of a coma, we witnessed the Lord's work over and over again. Now, I needed to forgive myself and stop beating up on myself for living out of God's will and fight my way back to Him totally. Many weeks passed, and she remained in the coma. I continued to live at the hospital, refusing to go home. I asked my husband to care for our five-year-old son. My staff and friends were great helping care for him. He would visit me at the hospital daily, and we would read and take walks. After about three months the hospital finally convinced me to leave and take a mental break for my own sanity. I decided to go home to bathe and spend a few minutes with my son. While I was running the water, the phone rang. My husband was on the other end. "Your daughter wants to talk to you," he said. I thought he meant she was restless because I left the hospital and needed to hear my voice to calm her. She would often thrash about the bed if she didn't hear my voice for a period of time. I was constantly talking and reading to her. My reply was for him to place the phone next to her ear and I would talk to her. The next thing I heard was a faint, crackly voice saying "Mom." I screamed, and with all of the excitement, the tub overflowed! So symbolic of God's grace. I rushed back to the hospital, and she was awake.

My daughter remained in the hospital until August. The hospital wanted to study her progress, since her case was one of the most severe head trauma survival cases they had seen. Hospital staff came to her room to talk to me daily, questioning me about my faith because her being alive was miraculous. They wanted to confirm this by asking me about Christianity. I witnessed to them about the goodness and mercy of God. I made sure everyone knew the wonderful splendor of our Lord and Savior.

Finally my daughter was able to come home, but she was blind in one eye and had many cognitive issues. The next medical step for her was to learn to walk, talk, sit, stand, and go to the bathroom again. The hospital suggested a nursing home. I refused by saying, "I taught her once, and the Lord will give me strength to teach her again." Physical, speech, and occupational therapy were the norm six hours a day for the next eighteen months. Eventually with the help of private tutors and special assistance, she was able to return to school, and today she lives a productive life.

The Lord put my younger sister Stacy in place to keep my business going. He positioned friends and neighbors to help in other areas of need. The Lord left no stone unturned. Tough days lay ahead. I had unfinished marital and business issues to handle. And there were situations with family members that were hovering in the wings. I was taking one day and one prayer at a time. Now, you thought I had a target on my life before this event? Well, the devil had a larger bounty out for me now! How dare I retreat to the one and only true living God and be under divine power and protection! Satan had me marked for destruction, and my mindset was working against me. Now that I was back on track, I became a larger target. Satan flees for a time, and he returns with a vengeance to try to reclaim and recruit.

The strain of my daughter's accident did nothing to help my marriage, so six months after the accident, I again asked my husband for a divorce. I still didn't fully understand marriage or commitment, and how God viewed marriage and divorce. I grew up under the curse of divorce and accepted it as a part of life. In the church I attended, divorce was one of the normal, yet sad results of a marriage gone wrong. You abandon the marriage and move on to a more suitable one. My interpretation of God's view on marriage was so narrow, and I bought into many views that were not acceptable to God. I was still focused on improving my life and ridding myself of a husband that I felt was not good enough for me. I did not seek God on the matter, because I honestly believed it was acceptable to divorce. Again, my husband suggested this might not be a good time to disrupt the family. Our family was trying to recover from a tragedy. I agreed for a while to just focus on the family. It was very difficult dealing with a man who had so much contempt for others. He would use harsh words like *hate* when referring to people he disliked. I was not comfortable being in a relationship with him any longer. It was just wearing me down with my daughter's recovery, a business, and a young son. I was picking and choosing my battles.

So much time had passed, and I still didn't know how to totally trust God with everything. It's a process that starts with studying the Word, praying for wisdom, and seeking God in all things. I was not accustomed to that.

The churches I had attended were more Sunday gospel-based and did not deal with Bible teachings or how to live a Christian life. I really had no excuse though. I should have been able to cling to God and allow Him to be my guide. My family had strong moral convictions; you just do what is right. That's the way it was—no support system, no point of reference. Everyone just did what was right in their own eyes, and dealt with condemnation when they failed. Divorce never felt right to me, but I didn't know where to go with those feelings. We tried counseling, but I was so convinced that this was just not the marriage for me. There were only a few marriages in our family at the time and divorce was very acceptable. I viewed all the older family members who were still married as old and so out of touch with the times. The enemy wanted that spirit of divorce to remain a part of our legacy.

I took a stand and filed for divorce. This was the beginning of a very long and bitter battle. When pride interferes with your judgment, foolish mistakes are made, and you err in attempts to use sound judgment. I allowed my husband to feel content in our marriage over the years when I knew my focus was elsewhere. I was ready to call it quits, but he was determined not to let his good thing end, at least not without a long, drawn out court and personal battle. I tried to remain focused, telling myself this was best for all.

This included keeping the children away from the battle grounds. I embarked upon a battle for my business and my self-worth. I was not going to allow this man to take my life away from me. No, this was not an option. I relied on prayer for my peace of mind and avoidance of bitterness. I never prayed for the marriage; I didn't know how. My experience with prayer was praying in hardship and prayers of gratitude for God's mercy and grace. I remember my grandmother praying daily, but I always assumed our prayers before God had to be in praise of his goodness or prayers of need in times of trouble. I viewed a failed marriage as just that, a failed marriage! I never understood that God instituted marriage and that all marriages are under God's authority. I always trusted the Lord; I never lost sight that all battles belong to the Lord. I waited and waited for the Lord to deliver me from this situation, and I assumed divorce was the ticket out. I had become the target for all the contempt my husband harbored in life. I thank God that I had such thick skin and a bull-head. The enemy meant it for harm, but God blessed me with a comfort level to withstand this battle with His peace. I never knew before how I was able to just ignore most of the verbal abuse and keep laughing and enjoying life. Now I know it was the Lord God, giving me His peace and joy and pressing me onward in my business and motherhood, happy and unaware of the impact verbal abuse had on most women. I was living in God's cocoon of protection and still blossomed in the midst of what takes a toll on most women.

When things like accidents, divorce, or illness occur, you sometimes find yourself left in a world of silence. This silence is the absence of friends, family, and the very structure on which you depended for some sense of security. You are left to reexamine your overall purpose and sense of being. You find out to whom your allegiance is pledged and for what you stand. I wanted a wholesome life and believed in everything good and mighty—One greater than myself. I wanted so desperately to live this life and fell so short in the process. I had been sidetracked time and time again for so long. With all the drama in my life, I was drawn to happiness, joy, and peace that only come from walking with God. I had no idea how I would get there, but knew it was available. I knew there was more than my life had become. There had to be examples for me to follow. I was beginning to realize that not all churches were structured to administer the gospel of Jesus Christ, or to disciple its members. I needed more to grow in Christ.

I was divorced after a four-year battle, and I know the Lord sustained my family during this process. The Lord brought many things to the surface. I still struggle with having caused another person deep pain. I know that God is the healer of all pain, and I hope one day that my ex-husband can forgive me and allow God to heal and restore him to a fulfilling relationship in Christ Jesus.

I'm just so thankful for the wonderful manner in which my children, especially my son, mentally processed the divorce. He allowed the Lord to penetrate his life early through Christian education, and he has never abandoned his walk with Christ.

Reflections

I have written about my divorce, and I'm not sorry to be out of a marriage that was full of bitterness. But remember that God instituted marriage, and all marriages are under His authority. If you are married, you should remain married, and allow the Lord to heal your marriage and become the driving force in your marriage. Seek godly counsel, and work hard on your relationship. There are so many great biblical resources to help couples succeed. Unless you are being physically abused or there is repeated adultery with no repentance, divorce according to the Scriptures is not allowed. Seek Christian counseling, get in a Bible-based gospel-teaching church, and allow God to be the center of your marriage. In cases of abuse, protect yourself and your children with every legal means available in your state. Each person's situation is different and should be carefully considered and based on godly principals and knowledge of all the facts. Be mindful that God is in control. God can make even the worst situations turn to good for His glory.

There was so much bitterness and hardening of my heart, and I didn't deal with it well. I was worn down by the trials of my daughter's accident and keeping family relationships going. And again, I didn't seek God's help as the controlling force. This marriage was based on the wrong foundation. My ex-husband's perspective of God was distorted by his ego and prideful outlook on his own abilities. We both had a hidden agenda in our marriage, and it was never God-based.

If I had to do it all over again, I would have done many things differently, but I don't allow myself to think any further than that. I do know had God been in our marriage it would have been saved. I am happy and praise God for where I am today, right now in the midst of His favor and blessing. Many of my struggles came from not knowing God's Word and living by His laws, and instead I followed man's ways.

1. How has this chapter caused you to reflect on your own struggles? Where do you see evidence of God in these struggles?
2. Can you identify specific provisions the Lord has made on your behalf that might not have been revealed to you until years later?
3. Do you keep a journal of God's provisions to track your growth in Christ Jesus?
4. Do you see yourself as a person willing to suffer to walk with Christ?

Reunited

inally I realized that the Lord had not left me, but I had left Him. I used to foolishly tell myself that I only left the church, not God; but the church is the family of God. I had a longing, but I was fearful of rejection and judgment from others. I was ashamed to admit my failures and lack of knowledge in the Word of God. It felt good for my commitment to God to be restored, but there was still the struggle to find a church where I could learn more and become closer to God.

I began to rely on doing things to keep me busy and in the will of the Lord. I wanted to foster a new attitude that was not about me, but about the divine purpose and will of God. To know that this life was preparation for eternal life and that true happiness resided in knowing and living the Word of God gave me rest. But focus on the big picture was now important; I needed to be sure to gather solutions for life's situations from biblical references. Trust in the Lord allowed me to become a successful, single parent with a thriving business to maintain. My strength, and help came from the Lord.

During trials, I had a tendency to feel a bit sorry for myself. All the negative things that had happened in the past and how they could have posed lifetime stumbling blocks kept coming to mind. Forgiving myself for my past and moving forward in Christ was difficult. I now realize that these were still footholds of the enemy in my thought life. But then, I couldn't see that the struggles were victory in Christ and preparation for what was to come. The process of God's preparation cannot be hurried, but yet I felt the need for wisdom in Christ in a hurry. I held on praying and hoping a path for me would be revealed soon. It just felt like I was in limbo. I longed for the Lord's help and divine guidance, but was often frustrated with waiting. In the past when I took on all the responsibilities of my life, it turned into such a pile of rubbish. I wanted to wait on the Lord but needed the blessing of patience to do so. Living in fast-pace society is difficult; we want everything to be quick. I wanted "parting of the Red Sea" miracles daily.

All the stress and pain was overwhelming and I wanted to avoid it. Hadn't I gone through enough? Where was my time-out? I get it now, Lord; can't I just rest in your blessings and never see another day of discomfort? I still wanted to make deals with the Lord and wanted God to be my personal butler on call whenever I needed Him. The big picture was still not clear to me. My "whining child" old self was beginning to resurface. These tactics hold very little success for children, so what made me think it would be attractive for adults? I still had a lot to learn about the Almighty God. I could just bite myself for some of the very immature methods of communication I shared with God. God was probably looking at me in the same manner I viewed my little children when they had tantrums—look and walk away and wait for it to end and then administer the proper response. Where were victory and reward without any discomfort?

More and more frequently, scriptures came to mind. This was a new experience. I can hear words from Job expressing how we only want to accept good things from God; we are so unwilling to suffer. However, these verses always convict me for a short time; then I am back to my selfish thinking. It takes several lightning bolt jolts from scripture to clear my head and get me refocused on God's purposes. The Lord has blessed all of us daily with such great benefits, but these blessings can work against us when we are not focused properly. All of our skills and abilities must be used to the glory of God. We have to remain willing to allow the Lord to use us. Seek Him, wait on Him, and, by all means, hear and obey Him.

God works in His timing, and not ours. The Lord will always deliver a solution. It may not come in the form we expect, but it will be on time and perfect in every way. Our job in the process is to remain prayerful and concentrate on how we weather the situation. Be a light to others and bear witness to our weakness so glory will come to God. We often keep silent when God could be glorified. Our praise magnifies the Lord's presence in our lives to the world. It's really difficult to remain focused in a world that has so many options and opportunities because at every turn in life there is something to take our minds away—families, jobs, and hobbies. We must remain busy with God's business—the business of serving others. Time must be spent praising God, and serving and teaching others about the kingdom of God. If we fail to take care of God's business and His people, all sorts of temptation will enter. We allow bills and laws to be passed only to wake up and find that prayer has been removed from the schools and marriage has been redefined—just to name a few.

In trusting God and His Word, we are obligated to place ourselves in positions to influence and shape the world around us by spreading the gospel and love. I began to allow God to reshape my life, but this was not easy for me. I had called all the shots for years. At least I thought I did. God had to retrain me, and I had to commit myself to being molded by God. What a mess! I was a broken sinner. Even with all my intelligence, I had no idea how far out of the will of God I was. My casual experience with the gospel didn't allow me to understand how grace and mercy manifest in our lives. I began to allow the Holy Spirit to rest, rule, and abide in my life.

God took the blinders off, and I could see so many things clearly for the first time. God's grace and mercy had been ever present in my teen years through my prayers of crying out to Him in pain from my awful childhood. I saw how He had kept me from so many downfalls that others have experienced. Now I see myself as God sees me, and my total hope is in Christ. Even though I was divorced and a single mother, my happiness came from Christ and I had so much joy in serving others. This spiritual gift of service gave me the wonderful life I had always wanted.

The years passed quickly, and soon I was in my mid-thirties. Again I had thoughts of marriage and possibly more children. Statistics and my age were against me, but I dared to step out in faith. Society wants us to believe that mid-thirties is old. People will say, "If you wouldn't eat a thirty-plus-year-old egg, why would you want to have a baby with one?" Our society just tries to shoot down all the greatness of the Lord. My dreams were strong and I certainly kept my options open. It was difficult to talk to anyone about my desires because I still had some reservation about being judged.

The Lord blessed me with great business endeavors. My two children were dealing with life after divorce and doing well in school. I had confidence in Christ and was thriving in His mercies. Even during my darkness, I felt the light of God making a path for me toward Him. I was so determined not to settle for wants and desires but to wait on the Lord to bless me with the desires of my heart. There were many situations that seemed so promising for my future and I thank God for quickly revealing His will in each instance. I could be optimistic in the Lord for I knew that my prayers and obedience were a source of comfort and protection, and the will of God would manifest itself.

I was having the time of my life. God was showing me how to display the fruit of the Spirit and just enjoy life in His peace and joy. I had always been a happy, energetic person, loving and willing to go the extra mile to help others, and I was thankful to be out of a relationship that bottled up those gifts. It had always been easy for me to establish friendships, but my earlier insecurities would often damage those relationships. With all that behind me, I really loved the life God gave me. I still appreciate all the good and the bad; for out of ugly, God made beauty in my life. For the first time in my life, I believed I was okay in Christ Jesus. I knew God's love and sacrifice for me deep in my soul.

Prayer was the center of my existence. I still had not found a church home, but I was involved in several community groups and Bible studies. Prayer was the basis for everything I did. I had lived so many years without prayer and a relationship with God, so I just couldn't imagine going back to a life of emptiness. My friends were also growing closer to God. We held each other accountable, and God blessed us with the support of each other.

Life went on as usual when I met a very interesting, tall, handsome younger man, Jonathan. God-inspired our meeting. We learned later, after several conversations, that we had been praying almost the same prayer. He was divorced and had a son from the marriage. I wanted to take it slow and wait on the Lord, so we just communicated via phone for many months. We agreed to meet several months later on New Year's Day for lunch. The lunch went well, but I was still very apprehensive. It was important to be sure this was of God, so I had prepared many questions for Jonathan. I wanted to know if he believed in one God and that Jesus was the Son of the one and only living God. He confirmed his belief, and that was one hurdle jumped.

Since my divorce, I had had many years to reflect and to seek God. I still wasn't in a good Bible-teaching church, but was learning more from the Word of God than in previous years. I prayed for wisdom and clarity as I dove into the Word of God daily. I realized that divorce revealed the true darkness of my heart as a believer, and I wanted God's light to shine and remove all the ugliness in my life. I was ready to totally experience God in my life. The only way I was going to press forward in any relationship was with God at the helm.

Jonathan and I began to get to know each other better. We shared our failures and our aspirations for a future with

Christ. It seemed after many years of disappointment, I was beginning to gain insight into my personality and the issues I had in relationships and with relating to others in general. The Lord blessed me with His peace as I gazed into my inner person. God healed me and repaired my self image. I needed to make amends in relationships I had damaged or destroyed with my actions, words, attitude, or a combination of all of those things. When the Lord finally got my attention, I was blessed with the ability to understand and simplify His presence and purpose in my life. The view became clearer, and my willingness to travel an unknown course navigated by the Master Pilot was a sure, sweet surrender.

Only until I surrendered to the true will and Word of God would I become united with Him and His plans for my life into eternity. Surrendering was very difficult because of my own mixed heartfelt desires, emotions, and ideas. I had to abandon my thoughts and desires and allow them to be transformed into God's Word and desires for me. I found surrendering to such peace was as natural as breathing. Before I struggled with the transformation process, I fought against myself by creating a battle between my Maker and me. The enemy is the author of all lies and confusion. He planted ideas in my head and made me believe that I didn't need the presence of God to be all that I wanted to be. Only the Word of God can explain the ability to feel the presence of God. The only time success came was after prayer, submission, and surrendering to His will in spite of my feelings, wants, or desires. Only the Lord giving me power to achieve a goal or accepting an alternative to the situation at hand accomplished this.

I stopped caring about things people said or thought of me. I stopped trying to please everyone. I stopped trying to make people understand my point of view. These were worthless efforts. The Lord doesn't force us to completely understand Him, so why would I think that my viewpoint could reach the inner being of anyone's heart? The Lord needed to touch my heart and life before I could appreciate the uniqueness in other people's personalities, talent, beauty, advice, and lifestyles. Sometimes my view of others was very limited. I overlooked their inner qualities and beauty that had so often been overlooked in me. I always felt more at ease with people who had a deep passion and concern for others, people who internalized and identified with the pain and struggles of others. The Lord has given each of us many talents to share with others, and I never viewed myself as having any worthwhile talents. I was just willing to help out whomever and whenever there was a need. This made me a nice person but nothing special. I never gave God the credit for being the driving force behind my spiritual gifts, and I was never aware that spiritual gifts were of value in the kingdom of God. Now I understand the biblical humility my grandmother tried to teach me as she said, "Always value other people more highly than yourself."

Reflections

Many of the struggles in finding my way are associated with not having the biblical foundation and structure needed to build upon. Our creation by God was based on the family, the church, and the state/community—each having sovereignty and working somewhat independently of each other but all working together for God's purpose. The family is governed by the Word of God; the church teaches and does the will and Word of God; and the state governs the people and provides rules for order in a systematic manner. The breakdown of any one of these entities has profound effects on our society. The Lord gives us clear instruction on marriage and divorce; but too often we just choose to ignore them and make up our own rules to suit our needs and selfish desires. Jesus comes and upholds the law and reinstructs man in the ways of His Father in Matthew chapter 5 with regard to divorce and marriage, but we tend to overlook the parts of the Bible that convict us. God's commandments on marriage must be maintained by the church, and accountability must be established to prevent high levels of marital turmoil and erosion in our society. Those who God joins together with Him at the helm as He guides them through the struggles of life, portray a powerful testimony. He shines brightly in those marriages.

We must remember to pray, stay, and obey. I know that so often I forget to pray first. I tend to react to the situation, evaluate everything in my mind, and then if my processing has flaws—only then do I remember to pray. This is a struggle we will always have in the flesh. When I have fallen on my face in prayer in the beginning, God has always been there from the start. The collateral damage is significantly less. I believe it's a learning process—the praying and seeking knowledge and wisdom from God.

God also uses reminders of my brokenness and my sinful nature to point me back to Him. I am saved by Jesus. Jesus is all that I am not. Jesus is innocent; I am not. Jesus paid the price so I will not. I have been washed in the blood, cleansed by the blood, and set free from the ravages of sin. I have been guilty of hiding under the holy blood of righteousness, instead of living in Jesus's righteousness. When I look to my own righteousness, I fail every time. There is no good in my nature, only sin. No more hiding. I must accept accountability for all that I say and do.

1. The Word of God instructs us to seek God early and in all things. How can you put this into practice?
2. Why is seeking God so necessary for developing strong roots in Jesus Christ?
3. What were the results of a time when you didn't seek God first?
4. What were the results of a time when you allowed your faith in God to take precedence over the situation?

5. Think deeply about the differences in the process and outcomes of these two situations.
6. The practice of seeking God takes time. What are some things you can do to keep your focus on the cross?

I am still growing in the Lord—His ways, His Word, and His will. I am willing to face whatever life has in store for me, resting in God's guidance.

Determined

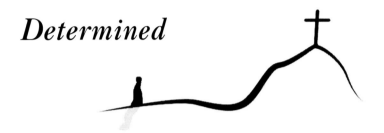

was in a strange but wonderful place in life—content and ready to receive divine blessings. After a storm has been weathered, the Lord has our attention, and we are ready to be blessed by Him. I wanted the Lord to bless my relationship and future marriage, but I knew it was important to do it the Lord's way and not the way society says we can. I was divorced, so I wasn't a virgin, but I still wanted to honor God by holding onto godly virtues. In the 1990's being over thirty with two children, if you tell a man you want to wait until marriage, it is not a popular statement. I don't think men hear that often, unless they are men of God. Worldly flesh had me conflicted, but God made my heart. I was determined to go with my heart and forget the world.

After praying and trusting the Lord, I believed that Jonathan, the very intelligent, humble man that I had met was God-sent. He responded to and met my needs and desires. He understood them as well as appreciated them. We begin to form a unity that seemed God-tailored. After five months of spiritual and financial counseling, we were married at my childhood church where my father was still a deacon.

Early in our marriage, we realized how alike we were, and there was a lot of "bumping of heads." I begin to seek advice and wisdom from God. Till death do us part? We were both stubborn type-A personalities. I saw myself in him and him in me. I now know that was oneness, but at that time it was pure frustration. I learned to be submissive and not speak or comment about everything. I began to make unfavorable changes in myself, but this was still not enough. Often looking at my husband was like looking at me, and we continued to bump heads. We were not able to remain in the same house during times of discussion and often needed a cooling-off period. This is one device of the enemy—to divide and separate. Things just didn't seem to be going the way we hoped or planned, so we started marital counseling from our church. We enrolled in classes to safeguard our marriage against divorce. We both were willing and determined to work at our marriage because we were in love and loved our life together. We were just experiencing some weak moments during transitioning into our new life together. We both were committed to the blessing of marriage.

I took on the task of making sure that I pleased everyone even at the expense of myself. Yet, we were faced with personality conflicts, blended families, anger management, and unresolved issues from his childhood. Even though these issues were serious, I can now look back and see that we took a casual approach in seeking out intervention. I wanted my husband to have the ability to confront and manage these issues. When things were good they were great, and when they were bad they were very bad! My husband was a wonderful man—I wouldn't have married him otherwise. Over 85 percent of the time he was just a dream come true, but there was that other 15 percent that was horrible.

In the middle of trying to establish our oneness in harmony, we were blessed to conceive two children. I was forty when our first was born and I had experienced cervical cancer and a myomectomy many years prior to meeting my husband. Our doctors gave us a less than 30 percent chance of conception with my medical history and age. Our family now included the daughter I had from rape, a son from my previous marriage, the child my husband had from his previous marriage, and now a daughter and son from our marriage. This seemed to complete the fairytale. I was still very determined to have it all, but in the process, I again forgot to place God first. I even placed my husband before

Almighty God. I got caught up in the blessings and forgot to give proper place and thanks and to remain steadfast in fasting and prayer.

I became so engrossed in motherhood and having babies with a man I was totally in love with. It was exciting to have a different twist on my life—an unexplainable natural high. Being super mom, wife, business owner, well-rounded friend, and more was the best! I wanted to be everything to everyone and not let anyone down. I planned the most exciting parties for both children and adults. It came so effortlessly I thought, but actually it came from God. Some of my spiritual gifts include hospitality, service, giving, and caring for others. God has a way of making service unto Him seem easy and natural.

Things were progressing very well. We had been taking marital classes at our church with other couples in various stages of their marriages. We seemed to get a handle on working together, and our marriage was growing and in bloom. But one day I woke up to a verbally abusive husband, and I tried to make sense of the situation. The skills and tactics that had been such a blessing in our relationship before were no long effective. The enemy was not about to allow marital bliss to reign. I had gotten lost in the needs of the children and overlooked a large part of my sexual ministry to my husband. I was so caught up in motherhood and working long hours in my business that exhaustion often overcame me. I didn't have time or energy for my husband. I was able to take the children to work with me, so I was with them all day. Even when I came home, I still devoted lots of time to the children, my household, and meal preparation. By the time it was evening, I would be too exhausted to even watch television with my husband. He began to have some mid-life crisis issues and started feeling neglected—rightfully so. He was unable to communicate all the things that were becoming a part of his thought life and his emotional struggles, so he was left totally frustrated. His place with me was occupied by the children. Our place with the Lord was occupied by everything that should never come before the Lord. We both were struggling with changes, balance, and priorities.

I believe we both saw and heard what we wanted to see and hear, and neither one took the other seriously. I was under the impression that we were going to be married for life, and a bit of a time-out to cherish motherhood and working was just not that big of a deal. I had waited my entire life for children with a wonderful husband that loved me and cherished me. Now that I finally had this life, I was going to enjoy it. I can see now how this caused my husband to lash out. Jonathan also started reliving some very painful and ugly childhood memories. I was unaware of the enormous baggage that he had been carrying around for years. I knew only bits of the abuse and poverty that contributed to his outbursts, but instead of going to the Lord in prayer for my husband, I thought the strong man I married would just pull himself up by his bootstraps. He was having trouble sleeping and his anger grew with intensity.

My thinking was so wrong and it was an invitation for Satan to enter and begin the destruction process. I still remained caught in the very full lifestyle we had. I was the owner of a thriving business, and worked at least sixty hours weekly if not more. My husband grew to resent my working and the business ownership. I believed I was placing God first and my husband second, but I was living in a deception of my own making. With every passing day, there was more lack of communication and lack of kindness in our marriage. I started to feel very unappreciated. We would still go out to lunch weekly, but I remember engaging in meaningless conversation and only going through the motions of marriage.

Over another year and few months, I noticed a drastic change in my husband. Our two youngest children were two and four by now. He made fewer attempts to engage in sexual activity. He complained more and put me down quite frequently. My desire for him sexually was so tied up in the way he treated me. It was difficult for me to welcome any advance. We both were turned off for various reasons and still unaware of how the enemy was operating in our marriage in the midst of our strife. Jonathan started going out with friends, which he never really did before in our marriage. It was always couples and an occasional stop off after work with coworkers, and I was always welcome to join them but I didn't very often. He loved sports and did the guy things. I trusted him and didn't keep tabs on his whereabouts.

I never imagined our deprived sexual relationship at home would make our marriage vulnerable. Physical attraction to other women while in a marital relationship had never been an issue for him. He always held himself to such high standards and I relied on him to maintain this at all times. Even now as I write this, it sounds ridiculous. My husband had self-control? Well where was the control when it came to the verbal lashing he dished out? Without God nothing is possible. I was so foolish!

If your relationship resembles mine in any way, I would suggest you refer to the Word of God immediately. Don't allow yourself to be taken in by the enemy as I was. We know the Word of God was written for us to obey and apply to our lives. In the Bible when David became bored and was on the rooftop looking at Bathsheba, he began to lust and allow his emotions and flesh to rule over him. I failed to see that this was about to take place in my life. I ignored several warnings from a dear friend about being too tired in the evening to attend to my man. I replied by saying to my friend, "Oh, my husband is not like that. He can go for months without sex." I was not aware that I was inviting the devil to enter my marriage by not being actively engaged in intimacy with my husband.

What I didn't know was that my husband had already been engaging in conversation with a woman. It started out as conversation to fill his lonely evenings when I crashed and burned early from a long day at work and with the kids, but it progressed from there. He had become more verbally abusive toward me and the children. We went to counseling at our church, but he was bitter and unwilling to participate. I began to pray a bit but still thought he would get it together. "It's just his past", I thought. I remember it was early September in 2004; I just couldn't take the silent treatment or verbal abuse any longer. I began to retaliate, so we agreed to separate. I still was unaware of his adultery. I just wanted to prevent things from getting worse. We both agreed that we wanted the marriage to work and divorce was not an option. Since you know Jonathan was committing adultery, I will share his reasoning for separating. I didn't know about the adultery; therefore, I didn't know he was feeling guilty about his betrayal and had been trying to break it off with the woman. She was threatening to tell me, and he was afraid of that. He assumed if he separated from me, she would no longer feel the need to threaten him. He would be free of her, and I still would not know. We could work on our marriage without me even finding out. I had no idea he was fighting his own demons, and the guilt was eating him alive.

Immediately after the separation, I just turned my life back over to God. I began to pray and fast and get into His

Word. It was difficult. My husband was still very bitter—trying to juggle me, the kids, and the spiteful woman. He was being taunted by issues of his childhood, his adultery, and his feelings of being neglected by me. He felt as if the Lord was calling him for something more, but he refused to heed to the call. During the years he had been attending church with me and the children, he had expressed an interest in doing more but never made the move. I played it safe and never pushed the issue out of fear of driving him further away from the church. He would tease and make fun of me because I was too religious. When he was young, Jonathan's mom took him to church. He was told about the Gospel of Jesus Christ and he asked God to come into his life, so he was baptized. He was given a Bible, but his mother stopped taking him to church.

By this time, the holidays were approaching, and my husband and I were in constant contact. He would come to the center to see our children daily. He was begging for help in the only way he knew how, but he was also blaming me for everything. Our children missed him, and we all were crying most of the time. I took a stand and vowed to walk closer with God. I took time off from work to read and study the Bible and I made time for daily prayer. I approached my husband several times and asked him if he was being unfaithful. He always said no. I was thankful that infidelity was not an issue in our marriage. I continued to pray and fast for restoration of our marriage. I could not believe that we were in this situation, but without God at the center of our marriage, I knew it was a roll of the dice. I was determined to weather the storm, not knowing that we were headed into the eye of a hurricane. I lost over forty pounds and countless strands of hair in just nine weeks. My husband was trying so desperately to make amends, but he was lashing out at me on one hand and on the other begging me to get him some help. He kept calling, asking me to help him. I was telling him to go talk to someone, but he was afraid for some reason. He grew angrier with me. He resented the fact that I had turned to the Lord, and he would tell me reading my Bible and praying would not help. I didn't know how to respond to him and I had no one to call to ask for advice. I just prayed and trusted the Lord to make a way. My husband became very angry with me for not comforting him, but I really didn't know what he expected of me. I had asked him to come home, knowing that the enemy wanted to keep us divided, but he kept saying no out of fear that his adultery would be discovered. One day out of anger with me, he called the woman to his apartment, and they had sex. Afterward he realized that he was in serious trouble.

I still didn't know about any of this. Later the next week, he was a different man. Christmas was approaching, and we managed to get through the holidays, communicating and making amends. I was equipping myself with the full armor of God and getting stronger in Christ each day. I was wounded but still committed to remaining in the battle. I was fighting for our marriage, knowing that my husband was not spiritually where I was, but I trusted God to be the binding force. With Christ I could face my failures and live the promise.

New Year's had come and gone, and it was finally Valentine's Day. My husband had planned to spend the day with me and the kids. I had been praying for the Lord to reveal to me the troubles in our marriage and show me how to fight to save it. I could feel a war breaking out, and I wanted to know what my challenges were. I had been fighting blindfolded, and I needed to know what the real issues were. I told God that with Him, I could face the truth and I was ready. God then revealed the truth to me. I received a call from the woman. She vindictively told me that she had been sleeping with my husband and gave all the dirty details. The pain I felt then was unbearable. How could anyone be so ugly and call me, the wife, after she had been so evil as to defile our marriage? I was caught off guard, temporarily. I regained my composure and remembered that a year earlier I was suspicious and confronted my husband, and he said no. So, I hired a private detective.

When the detective gave me the personal information on a young woman he said my husband was with, I immediately dismissed the idea, thinking the detective was trying to rip me off. I felt that there was no way my husband would have a relationship with a person like this.

I thought my husband had more honor than that. How wrong I was. I have to believe that the Lord was working even then to preserve my marriage for the future. I know had I believed the detective's information, divorce would have been definite. Even in my unfaithfulness to God, God remains faithful unto me. The devil is the author of all lies and deception. We fall prey to the enemy when we don't protect our thought life. We have to hold every thought accountable to the Word of God.

After the phone call from the paramour, I stopped to thank the Lord for his entire splendor. I had an enemy I was unaware of. The Lord took what the enemy meant for harm and started the process for a big blessing. That call, as painful as it was, was truly a blessing. After I was able to compose myself, I realized that my husband's soul and our marriage was the target. If we were not a threat to Satan, he wouldn't be bothered with launching a plan of destruction. I knew that the Lord must have big plans for our marriage and our service for His kingdom. After every successful battle, the soldiers are promoted. After the past few months, I was ready to be used and promoted by God. Here I was on life's battlefield fighting armed with an empty pistol, and the enemy had nuclear warheads aimed at me. Did I run and retreat? No, I filled my arsenal with the grace, love, forgiveness, and mercy of the blood of Christ, and I went forth with the mighty hand of the Lord leading the way. I dealt with it and faced the fact that infidelity is one of the enemy's biggest weapons and is the most effective. The only thing worse a man can do to his wife is take her life with his own hands.

If successful, Satan destroys the family, wife, children, in-laws, and friends with bitterness. I prayed and asked the Lord for guidance and took responsibility for my part in the marital breakdown. I was determined, with God's provisions, to get my family back together, and to bring my husband to a place where he could follow Christ and turn his life around. I knew that if Jonathan made a choice and asked for Jesus' forgiveness, he would be washed in the blood of the Lamb and follow Him, and he would become the man God created him to be. It had always been easy for me to forgive. This, however, would test that blessing. After I cried for a few days, hurt for a few more days, and then said "woe is me" for a few more days, I licked my wounds and returned to the battle. I knew this would be a cross to bear, but God's grace was sufficient enough. Now, this is where God struts His stuff. This was about the covenant between my man and me. God never breaks a covenant. God gives us instructions for divorce, and He also gives us conditions. I didn't need those conditions since I wasn't getting a divorce. The Lord had been preparing me for this battle even prior to my knowledge. I was armed, ready, and standing on the Word of God and waiting to see His mighty salvation. The Word of God contains all that I needed to survive the ordeal.

Before I took my stand, I repented and acknowledged that I had played a big part in the marital strife and lacked participation in God's design for marriage. I didn't honor God and make him the head of our lives and marriage. I didn't give honor to my husband as the head of our union. I had everything out of order and forgot the priorities—the authority of God, then honor and respect for my husband, and finally nurturing my children. I was even reminded of the hurt I inflicted on my spouse in my first marriage. In my first marriage, I felt my ex deserved every miserable thing I could say and do to him for the verbal abuse he heaped on me so often. I sowed seeds that damaged my future. Every deed that is sown reaps a harvest.

The consequences of sin can be long lasting. David's sin with Bathsheba caused pain for David throughout his life, including enduring the death of their son. I truly pray that everyone I have ever hurt for any reason is blessed with the peace and comfort that only comes from the Lord. Pain is pain no matter what the source. After experiencing so many levels of pain in my life, I give witness that only a life with God can be redeemed. I let the Holy Spirit take over and guide me to do the work that God has designed me to do. As a helpmeet to my husband, it was my responsibility to intercede in prayer on his behalf. I learned to pray for hours and in the name of Jesus rebuke negative spirits. I allowed the Holy Spirit to use me to be a vessel so that my husband could follow the light to repentance, forgiveness, and the wonderful salvation of God.

I knew that there was a blessing in the midst of this storm. But many friends who were praying with me when they thought my husband was experiencing a mental illness, ran for the hills when they found out it was adultery. There is such a lack of accountability among Christians. We would rather point fingers and pass judgment and pretend we have it all together than admit the truth—we are all flawed. If we aren't, then there would have been no need for the cross.

God has blessed our marital challenges by comforting our children and keeping them grounded and protected in His love. I continue to pray and fast and make sure I remain focused and grounded in the Word of God. I have made many changes in my life and my husband is still working on his relationship with Christ. God is allowing us to experience the full joys of marriage. It has taken prayer to sustain me and to keep my emotional hurts from interfering in our marriage. It's difficult some days, but with God I manage to prevent my unease to disrupt our marriage. I know the guilt and shame my husband feels, and God has blessed him to work endlessly to show himself as a man who loves and obeys the Word of God. The splendor of God is that we can turn from our evil ways, and he is just to forgive and restore. We don't have to live condemned. We are the righteousness of Christ Jesus. Unfortunately, among our family and friends, it's not that easy. My husband and I are judged and outcast and the target of lies, all because I remained in our marriage. Just know when you stay and give glory to God, your family and society may tell you to get out. I urge you to seek God, get some spiritual counseling, and stay your course. Yes, divorce is an option if you want it to be, but staying is a blessing and dynamic testimony of faith.

I will never regret being in the will of God. There is no other place I'd rather be.

Reflections

All the spiritually wise people will instruct you that marriage should not be entered into light-heartedly. That advice should also be applied to any thoughts of ending a marriage. God doesn't break a covenant ever, and we should remain faithful in our covenants as Christ Jesus instructs in His teachings. Marriage between a man and a woman is ordained by God. If you are faced with difficulties in your marriage, seek the help of your pastor, provided he is a man of God and is teaching the true Word of God unedited. I had an unfortunate experience in this regard. I went to the family minister who married us, and he said that because he looked into my husband's eyes and saw no light, there was no hope for our marriage. At this point, I knew in my heart by the Spirit of Christ in me that this was not my God speaking to me in such unfamiliar terminology. The God I knew gave hope in the midst of darkness and spoke words of life and light, not despair. This minister allowed these words to roll off his tongue so effortlessly as if he knew what only God could know. I trusted in my God-given spirit, and got as far away from that church as possible. I knew we needed to get involved in a real Bible-teaching church with Bible-practicing folks. We searched for a church home and never stopped believing and seeking the Lord in all His mercy.

We found another minister during our religious marriage counseling. This minister was willing to help until he witnessed firsthand the difficult personality my husband could display. He was offended by my husband's anger and vulgar comments. After a few weeks of counseling, this minister also said that my husband was a lost cause and that I should cut my losses and end things now. Again, we left that church a bit in shame, and I was questioning my every decision over the past few years. I never felt hopeless, but I did feel drained and struggling to find balance with my trust in God and my hope that all would be well. There was very little encouragement from my husband who was struggling with his guilt and many events resulting from his adulterous actions.

God was constantly in my face, never allowing me to give in to the pressures surrounding me. My help came from the Lord in many directions. My transformation began when I allowed myself to stop looking to man for what only God can give.

My focus had to remain on God and his Word and promises. I had to reevaluate family, friends, and even church membership. I had advice from many angles—professional, spiritual, and just plain busybodies. I learned that so many of us hide behind our titles and degrees, making every attempt to prove to the world, and sometimes ourselves, that we are worthy of greatness. We fool ourselves into thinking we deserve an honorable mention in society, never asking ourselves why we should be revered as upstanding/outstanding members of the human race. We seek leadership roles and admiration as we wait for our moment of recognition and adornment for our accomplishments. All along we are broken, flawed, and sinful individuals who turn our backs on our fellowman and kinsmen. In silence we delight at others' failures that allow us to stand out as complete. We quietly bring to light the mistakes and misfortunes of those that would benefit more from our mercy and compassion. We seek recognition at every turn in life—our education, jobs, marriages, children, homes, community service projects, and church involvement. We seek and appreciate quality and luxury for the wrong reasons. We separate ourselves from common happenings—the political unravel of our country and world. We distance ourselves from the hardship and suffering of those around us to gain superior status. We propel our egos into a state of denial, thus leaving us vulnerable to idolatry and self-righteousness. We misrepresent our Christianity and plain old-fashion values of humanity, love, caring for our neighbors, and seeking out godly ways to help all God's creations draw nearer to the cross. We are selective with our talents, gifts, and treasures; we place conditions on our service.

1. How can you live in the righteousness of Jesus and still maintain humility?
2. What are your challenges in standing before the world with bold faith in humility, modeling how to live life in Christ?
3. Think about some situations in your life when society's influence out weighed a godly perspective.
4. What daily practices can you implement to help you remain focused on who you are in Christ?
5. Think of a time when the Holy Spirit clearly caused you to change your choices and your course of action.

So often when we suffer a loss, only then do we return to the familiar place of comfort, principles, and a value system that never fails—God and good old-fashioned biblical teaching of love, forgiveness, and mercy. Why must we suffer before we allow our minds and hearts to gain access to what we know is the foundation of our existence? Only through God is this life possible, and only through

God can we gain greater wisdom into our very creation and purpose. By denying our brokenness and sinful nature we deny Jesus and the cross.

Blessings

Our Lord is an awesome God. He forgives, and His grace and mercy are magnificent!

I prayed for the Lord to come into my life and make changes where they were needed. It was necessary to ask for forgiveness and healing and for the Lord to show me His will for my life and marriage. I prayed to the Lord to heal my marriage and to start with saving me from my worldly ways. I prayed and fasted daily and asked for wisdom and guidance. The comfort I received from the praying and fasting and walking closer to God is beyond words. The Lord gave me, a broken vessel, a sense of belonging and purpose. The Lord reminded me that the battle had already been won, and that the victory belonged to Him. The Holy Spirit helped me to understand my job was to pray, fast, and wait, and God's job was to answer my prayers in the provision of His will. When it seems as if there is no answer from above, we need to seek God's will and His kingdom first then wait for everything else to be added as God sees fit to give.

I fell before the Lord seeking His mercy and forgiveness with my humble apology. Without realizing it, I had placed my husband before Him. The enemy is so clever. I allowed myself to get caught up in the things and affairs of this world. The rich blessings of a loving husband and the family that I had always prayed for were so enticing to revel in. I put my husband's strengths and character above God's, and when trouble surfaced, I relied on my husband's skills as a mere man to come through. The superficial makeup of a worldly description of marriage enamored me instead of causing me to fall on my face in prayer. Marriage is designed and defined by God and no one else. No more will I be deceived with the world's distorted picturesque views of God's creations. Christ is the Rock and foundation for our marriage and for all our family's needs.

I had abandoned all sense of accountability, but I thank God for never leaving or forsaking me. To be left in foolishness without hope or promise is a life I refuse to return to. The devil is not about to steal my joy or rob us of our marriage.

God says if we lack wisdom—ask, pray, and fast, and I did just that. In addition, I gained knowledge by reading the Word of God along with spiritual books on marriage, infidelity, and men's issues. I prayed for my husband, our family, and myself. I prayed that my husband would repent, be filled with God's Spirit, and have the mind of Christ. It took an investigation of my husband's childhood for me to really begin to understand all that he had endured. The Lord encouraged me to keep pressing forward at every horrible uncovering of the truth. At every discovery of the horror my husband endured at the hands of his mother, father, and stepfather, God's grace was sufficient. Over many months my husband was cleansed from the evil that haunted him for too many years. As each evil deed was brought out into the open, there was an overwhelming sense of God's grace and mercy through my husband's life. God was faithful to sustain him until adulthood under situations that have destroyed many others.

Looking back on the unfolding of many events in our marriage I know that God protected me as he navigated me back to Him. Had I learned of my husband's betrayal sooner than I did, our marriage may not have been saved. The Holy Spirit gave me blinders to lead me in a direction of accountability and not blame. God allowed me to see my own sin and brokenness first instead of my husband's. I had placed my husband in the number-one spot where only God belongs. I expected my husband to guard my heart and to control my happiness. What a fairytale! My husband had always believed in the Lord, but he was still seeking confirmation. He had never fully understood what living a life in Christ looked like. Now as I write, it is clear that this applied to my life as well. I had full knowledge and understanding of God and Jesus, but my application was quite foggy. I was neither a reader nor a doer of the Word. My disclosures here are not to belittle my husband but to show the power the enemy can have when we build our trust and understanding on the softness of this world. It is on Christ, the solid rock, we stand. God gives us specific instructions and even warnings. The intense way God loves us is so humbling. He tells us that we, His people, shall perish because of our lack of knowledge; but He also tells us if we lack wisdom we need only ask Him.

I feel very silly; suffering many difficulties because of my unwillingness to throw myself into God's perfect and wonderful plan and just remain delighted in Him for my blessings and desires. The Lord blessed our family in spite of our best efforts to sabotage what has proven over the test of times to be a flawless blessing. I managed to derail one the most desired and greatest blessings from God. Now I appreciate living in God's grace, mercy, and light. The Lord has gently led me to a place of forgiveness and healing.

We have experienced the support from sources that we would have shied away from years ago. We formed prayer groups and surrounded ourselves with other married couples that have achieved success in marriage by giving way to the Word of God. We are allowing our life, marriage, and family to be defined by the Word of God, not defined by decaying morals of this world. We take no comfort in this world, because we know that this is not our final destination. We are in preparation for eternal life with God. All that we are and have are on loan from God to work His plan and will for our lives and the advancement of His Kingdom, not for our simple satisfaction. Our unwise use of our time, gifts, and talents contributed to allowing the enemy to gain a foothold. We know we must live up to the fullness God has placed in us all for His glory. God has made provisions to equip us to have all the things He created us for. We must live within the covenant, keeping the law and being saved by grace. Our lives and works should reflect Jesus. Love is truly defined by the Word of God. He loves us so much that He gave us His Son. God will not allow our sins to separate us from Him if we know Jesus. Trusting God and meditating on His Word and works will get us to the forever after eternal place.

Reflections

As I look back over my journey up to this point, I am fully engulfed by the magnitude of God's love for us. In my darkest hours I was so full of joy and comforted even during our separation. This was a delightful time for me. I could feel the Spirit of the Lord working in our lives. I was being personally trained by God to live a better and more fulfilled life. I was reestablishing godly order and obtaining a new appreciation for my husband with the correct outlook. All the things I loved about my husband's character were of God. Even though life with him has been difficult, I've seen the Lord manifest Himself in many ways. Our marriage has undergone much turmoil only to put us face-to-face with our sinful nature and with Christ our Redeemer.

Each person and each marriage will face its own set of challenges. God's grace and mercy will come in and sweep the dirt away. A new path will be lit, and God will restore you to a place of biblical miracles. Sometimes we think of miracles as only happening in the days in which the Bible was written. We associate our lives with the world because we are immune to God—so we fail to see that each day is a day that the Lord gives or takes. God cares so much for us, He leaves nothing to chance. He has prepared every issue in life we will be faced with. We need only to remember to seek God earnestly, obey His Word, and apply it to every aspect of our lives. Nothing is possible without God. We need to recognize God as our number-one priority and hold every thought captive to Him. Cast out all evil thoughts and deeds in the name of Jesus, and know that for every deed there is a seed. We will be held accountable for sowing and reaping from the life we live. There will be a harvest and our participation, whether in the will of God or not, will determine the outcome of our actions. Even though God is just to forgive and save; we face earthly consequences for our sins. God is blessing my family right now to deal with our consequences as we walk and serve Him. In Christ Jesus we can live without condemnation and hold our heads high in His love and sacrifice knowing that we are forgiven, set free from sin's bondage, and set aside to live with Christ forever. Until then, it is by His grace we are living in the presence and favor of God.

God has blessed our family with a pastor and church following His teaching and with a support system that holds us and our commitments accountable to the Word of God. We believe God is the head of our lives; His will comes first. God is the head of our finances, and he gets the first ten percent. God is the head of our marriage. His plan for marriage comes first. God has given us our children and we are to raise them under His covenant. God is in us as we work on our jobs and provide services in the name of God. God is in us as we communicate and relate to our friends and family. God is in everything pertaining to life here on earth and in heaven. As our pastor reminds us, God is first in all things.

1. What are some daily practices that could help remind you to seek God's wisdom and advice at the beginning of each day so that he will always be placed first?

2. In the past I gave God the leftovers at the end of the day. With whatever energy I had left, I would

put forth a tired effort to read His Word. What about you?

3. Try thinking back in your life to a year ago. If you are journaling, you can read a page from last year's writings.
   - What was going on in your life then?
   - Can you immediately see God's work in your life since then?
   - Have you witnessed changes in the people around you?

4. Now try thinking way back to 5 years ago (or reading from your journal.)
   - Compare then to now
   - What favor and provisions has God given you?
   - Was there a blessing from God in your life then, but you just couldn't see it?

5. What are you most thankful for today as you reflect on your past? Consider both the negative and positive things that have occurred.

When an angry person allows God to redirect his focus and passion on matters for the Lord, that person becomes a dynamic tool for Christ. His works bring glory to the kingdom of God. If you are an angry person, give that energy over to God to harness and unleash for His purpose. God will use your light to bring attention to how He— Mighty God can save.

Mountain Climbing

*A*s I climb the mountain of faith and gain strength and wisdom in the ways of the Lord, I have learned not to rely on my own understanding. I trust in the Lord for all my needs and desires. I'm delighted to stand in my salvation and wait on the will of God. I choose to live grounded in His Word and bask in His glory all while praising God Almighty. So often I failed to worship and praise God. I was so busy asking for things and wanting things, that I sinfully related to God as a means to get stuff. Then when all our stuff is gone or offers little satisfaction, realization appears quickly in the midst of darkness and despair. Praise and thanksgiving takes on a meaning of larger proportions.

If mountains were smooth they would be impossible to climb. The rough bumps we experience as life's trials serve as tests, reminders, and lessons to gain access to greater exposure to God's plan. Wisdom is gained at every turn. And when biblical application is practiced, life in Christ takes on a meaning that can only be understood and appreciated with the full understanding of who God is.

One would think that during this process I was discouraged. To my amazement, in Christ Jesus I was comforted, entertained, and encouraged to press forward. My concern for what others thought and said was buried far in the back of my mind. It was easy to remain focused in my faith, but my focus didn't render me exempt from Satan's attacks. I was ridiculed by family and friends. Many claiming to be Christians made great attempts to discredit my husband and spoil our blessings in Christ. There were times when I would entertain the notion that my husband was not worth all of the anguish, but I quickly felt the strong Spirit of the Lord bring correction to my thoughts. It was not about my husband's or my worth and value. This was about God and His will, His kingdom, and His glory. It was about a larger picture, one of God's will, a covenant relationship. It was about my service to the Lord. It was an example of brokenness, repentance, redemption, salvation, and life ever after. My worthiness and my husband's worthiness have already been established on the cross. Our attempt to measure worthiness is completely unnecessary, and warned against in the Word of God.

God directs us to form civilized systems to be governed by as we live on this earth. In this country our founding fathers based our governmental system on biblical principles. This system may be flawed since mankind is flawed, but it should be respected. As Christians we give honor to God as the Supreme Judge. Our laws and our churches are under the authority of God, and they guide us in being accountable. Our marriages and children must also be accountable to the authority of Christ Jesus.

Placing everything at the foot of the cross has been liberating for me. As I endeavor to reach the top of the mountain, I know that my husband, with the Lord's help and guidance, will have to deal with his childhood issues, adultery, his emotions, our family and children, work, and friends. I know this is not my burden to handle alone. I cast my burdens on Jesus who died on the cross for our sins.

Any specialized activities and sports require preparation and the proper equipment to ensure success. Immersing myself in the Word of God and particularly in the teachings of Christ is preparation to withstand life's trials. Finding a way to remain focused and serve others during my difficult times was comforting. During my darkest hours it helped to move my thoughts away from my situation and focus on others. Trusting the Lord leaves no opportunity to worry. When I allowed myself to worry about tomorrow I missed out on the blessing of that day. No matter what I'm facing, there is always someone who is in worse circumstances. I try to be salt and light for others to see God by just being content in my blessings and knowing God is in control. God will make all of the provisions needed for our situation. Pray and seek out confirmation before making attempts at a solution. At times God has blessed us with an immediate solution or blessing. Other times we have to pray and wait, and a blessing may come from an unlikely source by unlikely means. Taking everything to God in prayer was a practice-makes-better routine for me.

When my husband was out of our home, it freed up my time to care for others. For example, an act of kindness toward a sales clerk produces light. The same sales clerk will be in awe when you remember a personal detail about her life and show interest in such details. Serve by volunteering to assist others for no apparent reason. Cook a meal for someone ill or offer to clean for a senior. The list can be endless if you allow the Lord to direct you. In your giving, be humble. How we navigate through our difficulties is as important as our praise. It was easy for me to be bitter and hurt. After all, I was wounded, but I was still in the battle. Our method of trusting in the Lord is a reflection of our faith in God.

How can we get others to believe we serve a mighty God if we walk around sad, bitter, and angry during difficult times? Our faith in the all-powerful God should reflect even in bad times. We can't tell people how awesome our God is; we have to live in the splendor of an awesome God. Our talk, walk, and praise are beacons of hope to those blinded by darkness. As believers our lives should be different than those who are not believers. No words are needed.

If we keep reminding ourselves of God's laws, it is easier to remain focused. The world keeps reminding us that we have freewill, and there is a temptation to use our freewill without considering God's will for our lives. If we don't keep God's laws before us, we will become bombarded with the world's slogans all around us. The pressure of family opinions has no place in a marriage. I had to respectfully announce, "Unless you are repeating the Word of God, keep your opinions to yourself. I have enough of my own." My popularity among family and friends was replaced with criticism, judgment, and in many cases, down right rejection.

My husband was feeling the effects of his sin and was apprehensive to accept forgiveness, knowing that he was being judged and disowned. He knew that I was being tormented, and the enemy used guilt to paralyze him from feeling worthy of our family and my love.

I took this time to strengthen my relationship with God so when my husband and I started working on our relationship, we would know who we were in Christ and what we had in Christ. The preliminary issues would be out of the way, and we could get right down to being obedient to God's will. God was purging our weaknesses and replacing them with the mindset to serve Him. I should have been an emotional mess according to the world's view of how stressful times should be handled. I look back and know God was in control. I surrendered to the authority of my Creator and was able to hide myself in His grace and mercy. There I was comforted and encouraged by the Holy Spirit to press forward in Christ Jesus and not be concerned; just trust and obey.

In studying the books Esther, Daniel, Job, and James, I found confirmation of God's sovereignty in everything. In my most resistant state in life, God was just in gaining my attention and pointing me back toward a love I longed for. God's love is the only love that could comfort me long term from the ongoing consequences of my husband's actions. In the story of David, God forgives but reminds us that there are earthy consequences that spring forth from our sin. He will remain faithful to guide us as we deal with the outcome.

Reflections

In order to protect our children from certain information and details at this time, I'm going to be very selective about the information I disclose now. My husband and I both know that we will have to make them aware of consequences that will remain a part of our lives forever. My husband is gaining understanding and biblical application to his life. It's a blessing to give witness to the glory of God. Each day is a day filled with God's mercy and favor. Watching my husband and listening to him quote the Word of God and grow in Christ is a blessing and miracle. God is healing him of all the ugliness he suffered at the hands of his parents. Watching God redefine him in the image of God and not his genetic make-up is awesome. The thrill of our future being grounded in Christ is a heritage we can leave our children. Sharing our faith has become a big part of our daily routines.

During a storm it is easy to become involved in our own circumstances, but in Christ we are much more than our situations. Our circumstances can become a direct reflection of the complete sovereignty of Almighty God, showing Christ's power and love.

1. During your most difficult day this next week, stop and do something for someone else. Then reflect on and write down how you were blessed.
2. Give to another person what you think you most need at that time. For example, if you are in need of free time, become a blessing to a friend/relative by offering them a night out without their children. Then reflect on the blessing.
3. When you have financial challenges, give more than your tithe, or give someone a gift card or flowers.

Take the focus off of you and be of service to others allowing the Lord to work through you. If we wait for the ideal time to serve others, we will miss many opportunities and blessings to bring glory to a big and mighty God.

Study, prayer, and service make my days brighter no matter the seasons or the weather.

Peace in the Valley

There is peace and joy in Christ Jesus. I rejoice knowing that all my debts have been paid. I have been purchased with a price that was too high for me to ever repay, and I have gained my freedom to live eternal life with God. All my life's journeys have been preparation for the kingdom of God, and all my experiences have shaped me into the person God can mold and use to His glory. When I tell of my brokenness and others see my transformation, they will know there is a God. No matter what life brings my way, I can and will survive in Christ Jesus. The pressures of society don't exist anymore for my family or me. We have been lower than an ant's belly, and the only way out was for us to look up. My fears might have consumed me, but by the grace of God, I'm here to give testimony that God never fails. My total and complete surrender to the perfect, incorruptible will of God has given me a feeling that could never come from marriage or motherhood. We were created by God for God. When we operate out of the will of God, we will always be on a sinful quest to fill our lives with empty, meaningless stuff, people, and things. Living in Christ and keeping God's law puts us in direct line to eternal life. Until this life is over, we live under the divine will and protection of Christ Jesus. God provides the water to make it a bit easier to swallow the large jagged pieces of life. I urge all to beware of evil. If we tolerate wrong, we will become immune to its ill effects. In order to recognize evil when it appears, remain prayerful and live in the Spirit. God gives us specific instruction on how to address every situation in life. We are emotional beings, but we also have the tools and a guide to deal with and handle these things. We are reactionary, emotional creatures, but we can control our actions according to our faith in God. We really don't have to respond to evil or negativity. We can simply pray and rely on the wisdom of God and allow the Almighty to handle situations that attempt to bring harm into our lives.

So many times I would turn a situation over to the Lord, but when the opportunity presented itself for me to make a statement or react, I would. Well, my actions prolonged the victory, and resolution took longer. The more I tried to handle the situation, the more I was conveying to the Lord that I was in control and not Him. Being still has been one of the most difficult challenges of my spiritual journey. Total surrender and waiting on the sidelines has never been one of my areas of strength. It's funny how getting kicked around on the battlefield will leave you with a few lumps and send you running to God. I thank God for giving me a spiritual father and grandparents who exposed me to the truth. I could still be lost and on a journey to nowhere, but instead I am on my way to meet the King.

There is so much comfort and peace in being in the divine will and protection of the Lord. As for me and my house, we will serve the Lord. During this process, our children have learned to pray and trust God for the best outcome. When our children had questions, I remained faithful to God to give them an answer from the Word of God. I let them know that my abilities in Christ Jesus were clearly defined and that God was in total control. They could see how, in Christ, we can be comforted and our joy and peace is solely Christ Jesus. They have learned early in life to maintain a prayer life pleasing to God. We are teaching them to take everything to God in prayer. Our hopes and prayers are that these covenant children will learn to trust God and obey His Word and apply His laws to their lives. We want our children to be strong in their service and commitment to working for God. With God, we are teaching them to deal with the ways of this world knowing that they are not to conform but be transformed by the Word and power of God. We can give witness to our brokenness when the time is right and show them God's faithfulness unto us. We can leave them a legacy of a strong marriage in Christ. We can give them hope in their faith in the midst of troubles. These are lessons best learned early. We are training our children up in the ways and practices of the Lord.

Our isolation from extended family has given us new perspective and insight into the ways of God and not man—leaving our parents and clinging to each other and being grounded in the covenant with God. If each family takes responsibility for its actions and is accountable to God, all will serve God more effectively. If God hadn't removed my husband and I from certain elements in our family, we would have still been struggling to please family members and giving an ear to their ungodly advice. My prayers for God's revelation freed me from a continuous cycle of being manipulated and teased with the promise of family contact upon total compliance. How twisted is man's absolute power over another. Instead of unconditional commitment to one another, we offer up our emotionally bankrupt lives, and in our flawed ways, try to carry out a personal agenda. It was painful to allow God to separate us from certain family members. My family life had biblical foundations, but there were many areas of dysfunction. After decades of conflict, God released me from my turmoil.

My husband's family life was horrible, but to the glory of God, He protected my husband in his younger years with coping skills. He managed to be a great student and attend college on an athletic scholarship. God was making long-term provisions well before my husband would ever suffer the ill effects of his disadvantaged childhood. During our separation, we could see God's work and favor. There is victory in Christ Jesus.

Trust God, invite Him into your life, and trust Him to make changes that will last.

Reflections

Maybe the following questions will help you think about ways to journey into your own "peace in the valley" through resting in Jesus Christ.

1. How many times do you wake up in the morning thinking of ways you can please others?
2. What are your views about serving God by serving others?
3. In your spare time, what are your favorite things to do and why?
4. Have you considered adoption or mission work?
5. How comfortable are you sharing your faith?
6. Are you willing to take classes to gain greater discernment into the Word of God?
7. Do you know the names of the cashiers at the stores you shop at the most, and do you interact with them?
8. How do you provide service to the poor and elderly?

9. What helps you during a life crisis?
10. Do you have friends that will give you Godly advice?
11. How do you allow God to comfort you?
12. What ten scriptures can you recall effortlessly to help you draw near to God in time of difficulty?

Victoriously Homeward Bound

I have victory through Christ Jesus. In the past I would pray and look for "parting the Red Sea" miracles, overlooking the everyday miracles that were a part of my life daily—our blessed union, our children born to a mother surviving cervical cancer, my youngest son whom God keeps safe daily when a single taste of tree nuts could end his life. I never worry when my son goes to school. I trust God to watch over him in a way I never could.

I can name numerous situations that are miracles from God. I guess I have to revamp my former statement. Saving our marriage in the way God did was a "parting of the Red Sea" miracle. My husband and I have a love that transcends every theory man can come up with. Our testimony is not filled with hours of therapy; but spiritual guidance from a Christian minister or therapist can be helpful. My husband allowed God to heal him of his past hurts, bring him to a place of repentance, and teach him the ways of the Lord. Love and commitment have been restored by Christ Jesus. I can love my husband in a much deeper and complete manner than ever before.

I can be the wife and mother that God has called me to be. My worth is measured by the cross—not by marriage, children, works, or financial success. With the help of God, I will not allow myself to fall prey to the lies of this world. I will remain focused on seeing myself as God sees me—in His image. I will define myself and my purpose as God does. Fasting and praying is always instrumental in gaining God's perspective. The more I position myself to be used by God the more victorious and blessed I am. During my trials, I delighted myself in the things that pleased God.

I'm sure by now you want a clear answer, about where my husband is and how things worked out. It should be no surprise to you that God is God all by Himself. He needs no help. We didn't need to drown ourselves in work, a bottle of medication, or counseling. I'm thankful to God for victory. We were separated for about ten months, but God brought us back together and He continues to heal both of us and our marriage. It has been a pleasure to wake up daily to reap the benefits of living a life with Jesus. We work hard to restore understanding in our marriage. We both trust only God to do what no one else can do. There aren't enough words in the English vocabulary to describe what God has done in our marriage. He has taken our love to greater levels. We are still faced with consequences, but our trust and faith in God will sustain us. We look forward to each day the Lord gives us together until death. We delight in God and His provisions and accept all the challenges that come with sin and salvation. We both can define our relationships with the one and only living God.

After many years of searching, seeking self-gratification, buying into the American Dream, and living in the flesh, I had to go back to the source, the beginning, in order to find what I needed and had been searching for. For me, the things I wanted were predicated upon the foundation that was laid before me. My parents set the standard that came from their parents and so on. These morals and principles were the Word of God.

I realize that the desires, convictions, and conscience I have are the Spirit of God that lives within me, guiding me to my Creator. The things that I longed for are the things that the Lord designed for me as well. However, I had been seeking these things in the wrong manner. My way of thinking was selfish and of the flesh, and I failed to include the Lord in His own plan for my life. I allowed virtue to take a back seat to self-indulgence and the social attitudes that "you can have it all." During this time of my life, I suffered unnecessary hardships and prevented myself from experiencing the benefits of a rewarding Christian life at a young age. I sold myself out to the flesh and the world. I denied God and denied myself the pleasure of being fruitful. What a wonderful God we serve that regardless of the circumstances, He is waiting and ready to forgive and receive us into His merciful arms when we turn to Him. To God be the glory—the author and finisher of my faith!

While I was running around searching for the ultimate bridegroom and planning the reception, I almost missed the wedding and the opportunity for complete happiness. The Bridegroom has been waiting at the altar since He died on the cross and rose from the grave with all power under heaven and on earth.

Only a life with Jesus can make us beneficiaries of God's kingdom in its entire splendor both here on earth and in eternal life. Jesus tells us that He came so that we can have life and have it more abundantly. Living with Jesus in my life, heart, and soul is living the ultimate life. My journey is complete, and my destiny is determined—a life with my Lord and Savior Jesus Christ.

I pray that everyone who reads this book will tell someone else about God's wonderful working powers. I pray that they will use my testimony to inspire, renew, and multiply their faith in God.

- Seek God in all His glory.
- Spend time alone with God daily, reading and meditating on His Word.
- Renew your faith, and be thankful for the cross.
- Demonstrate your faith.
- Praise God by sharing testimony to inspire others.
- Renew your passion for God's favor and provision.

I love you all in Christ Jesus, and thank you for allowing me to witness in the name of Jesus. Amen.